PERFORMANCE
BREAKTHROUGH

The Four Secrets
of Passionate Organizations

MIKE GOLDMAN

To Angela, Richie, and Jessica –

You make me strive to be a better person everyday.

INTRODUCTION

I've worked with dozens of companies over the last twenty years and, without exception, the largest opportunity for each and every one of them was the same. Big or small—from companies like Disney, Levi Strauss, and Polo Ralph Lauren to the local accounting firm, hotel, or plumber—the largest opportunity for improvement was helping *people* better realize their potential. New strategies, processes, and systems are certainly important, but people will trump them every time.

Recent Gallup Organization research concluded that only 29 percent of employees are truly engaged in the work they do. That means 71 percent of your employees are trying their best just to get through the day. It also means they would probably not think twice before leaving for a better, or maybe just a different, opportunity.

29 percent engagement! That's like an engine running at less than one-third power. How can a team reach its potential, or come anywhere close, with that level of engagement?

Imagine the impact of injecting more passion into your team. Imagine a company where eight out of ten people were truly engaged. What would this mean to your team's productivity, morale, retention, and ability to recruit top talent?

PERFORMANCE BREAKTHROUGH

Imagine a work environment where:

- ☑ You are not crushed by the stampede out the door at 5:00 p.m.
- ☑ Team members offer their help without being asked.
- ☑ Team members offer their ideas without being asked.
- ☑ Team members find ways to get the job done; not excuses for why they can't.
- ☑ Internal celebration replaces internal competition.
- ☑ Customer loyalty replaces customer satisfaction.

Realizing the opportunity of creating a more passionate workforce brings several challenges:

1. *The Next Big Thing*
   Companies make a considerable effort in looking for the next big thing: cutting-edge products, increased automation, new markets, and more efficient processes. However, they spend comparatively little time figuring out how to get a higher return from the most expensive resource they have…their people.

2. *Old-Style Management*
   Old-style management still prevails at many companies. Dictatorial environments where executives believe employees should be passionate about their jobs simply because they get a paycheck. Even in more forward-thinking companies, leaders know the dictatorial style no longer works but have never been taught how to truly lead people to get optimal results.

INTRODUCTION

When employees are asked what is most important to them, studies consistently show that money is not even in the top five. Things like the type of work, respectful treatment, opportunities, coaching, and development are most important.

3. *Multi-Generational Workforces*
   Four distinct generations make up today's workforce— veterans, boomers, generation X, and generation Y. While it's dangerous to stereotype, each generation has its own values, motivations, and work ethic. While this diversity can be a great strength for any organization, the reality is most companies fail to understand how best to take advantage of these differences.

The following quotes are typical of boomers:
   ☑ "These kids just want everything handed to them on a sliver platter. I can't seem to find a way to get them to work hard."
   ☑ "Doesn't anyone understand company loyalty anymore?"

The following quotes are typical of generation Y:
   ☑ "Why should I work my butt off for twenty-five years for one company when there are so many other good opportunities out there?"
   ☑ "I didn't go to school for seventeen years so I could just follow orders. There's more value that I can add, but no one will let me."

People don't quit companies, they quit managers. The days of iron-fisted managers who run their people into the ground but are rewarded for "making the numbers" are gone. These days, people, not factories or raw materials, are a company's most important resource.

How will you feel the impact of these challenges?

1. *Increased Employee Turnover*
    In any economy, new technologies and flexible work arrangements have given employees more choices than ever before; and, by the way, your best employees have the most choices, and therefore more reason to leave! Think about the impact that would have on your customers, employee morale, hiring costs, training, and the number of non-gray hairs on your head.

    If you haven't begun to see this problem in your organization, you will. If you don't tackle this problem today, you will pay dearly to solve it tomorrow.

2. *Increased Difficulty in Recruiting*
    Finding good people is difficult. Regardless of the current economy, baby boomers hitting retirement age will cause a shortage of people to fill skilled jobs. Most good candidates will have several opportunities to choose from.

    This will cause two types of problems: either your company will be understaffed as you wait longer to fill those open spots, or you'll rush to fill open spots by settling for employees that are not really qualified for the job.

3. *Low Productivity and Profitability*

   Most people who are not passionate about their jobs don't quit, they stick around and become the "walking dead." These zombies look like they're working but they probably top out at about 15 percent of their potential. What's worse is that negative attitudes are more contagious than positive ones. Poor morale is like a cancer slowly killing your organization.

This book contains the answers to these challenges and the promise of creating a more passionate, productive, and profitable organization. You'll find that the ideas discussed are not expensive to implement. In fact, many can be executed without spending a dime.

The book's message is communicated in the form of a fictional story to help make these ideas real and implementable, as opposed to fuzzy concepts. I hope you'll find it also makes for a more enjoyable read.

Mike Goldman
President, Performance Breakthrough

* * *

WHAT THE HELL HAPPENED?

My name is Andy Martin and success had always been a given for me—a job with a top consulting firm right out of college and a career rocket launch into space from there. Staff, senior, manager, partner…there was no stopping me. Traveling all over the country, working with Fortune 500 companies, it didn't get any better than that…except for the traveling all over the country part.

Three years ago I decided I'd had enough of parenting and husbanding (is that a word?) by phone. Being out of town Monday through Friday was getting incredibly old. It was time to start actually participating in my children's lives and spending some quality, unrushed time with my beautiful wife. Besides, I didn't need to work for someone else anymore. After seventeen years, I was an "expert." So why not start my own firm consulting wherever and to whomever I wanted.

Hence the birth of A.M. Consulting and the start of "the good life." Or, so I thought…

It's amazing how quickly you can go through seventeen years of savings and two lines of credit when you're really focused…and boy was I focused.

Things started off strong. A few local clients who I'd worked with at my previous job decided to give the new firm a shot. I hired six consultants and we were off to the races. We beat our plan each of the first twelve months and we were up to fifty employees before the glue was dry on our office nameplate. That's when the real "fun" started.

It's hard to see the floor falling out beneath you when you're running as fast as I was, but by the time I looked down, the fall was pretty steep.

It started when our largest client, who made up forty percent of our business, decided they wanted to go "in a different direction." I'm still not entirely sure what that meant or what new direction they were now headed. What I am sure of is that we would no longer be paying our bills with a portion of our biggest client's profits. It also meant I had twenty consultants "on the bench" (that's consultant speak for getting paid for doing nothing).

The fun continued when I informed those on-the-bench consultants that they now had to work on some business development activities (that's consultant speak for selling). Since, for some people, selling is a dirty word, within two months, half of my on-the-bench consultants decided to quit. Of course, they included a good portion of my top performers.

Over the next several months, we teetered on the brink of success and failure. Clients would come and go, employees would come and go, and our high growth business was shrinking by the month. The "rah-rah" attitude we started with was now almost completely gone. Employees weren't happy, clients weren't happy, and I wasn't exactly a thrill to be around.

This is where our story begins.

* * *

DOWN HILL

I arrived at the office 7:15 a.m. as usual. I was always the first one in and the last one out. I used the quiet time to work on things impossible to get to when employees and clients were awake.

That morning's goal was a new attendance policy. In consulting, it's important to be there when your clients are. That usually means you're in before they are and out after they're gone. We like to think it gives the illusion of non-stop work (although I don't think our clients are really that naive).

During our go-go growth days of year one, I needed to threaten people to get them to go home. By year three, you could be trampled if you were standing in the doorway at 5:00 p.m.

It was about 8:30 a.m. when the phone rang. It was John Simms, my director of business development. He helped me start the company and was basically my right-hand man. John and I knew each other for fifteen years. He joined Vincore Consulting (my old firm) five years after me. I became something of a mentor to him, but he was a quick study. After a few years, it was less of a mentoring relationship and more of a partnership. I made sure he was on my team for every important project. When I decided to leave Vincore, it was almost a foregone conclusion that he would come with me. When I was up to my ears in day-to-day problems, he was the one person I could count on to think strategically and keep us heading in the right direction.

PERFORMANCE BREAKTHROUGH

"Andy, it's John. Are you free to talk this morning? I need to speak with you."

This didn't sound good. "I'm free now, what's up?"

"I'd rather stop by your office and talk in person; will you be around in about thirty minutes?"

This really didn't sound good. "I'll be here. I'll see you then."

Any discussion that can't happen over the phone is usually bad news. John was leading the effort to get Vault Communications (our second biggest client) to start a big new project we had been proposing to them for the past four months. It would have meant a major new revenue stream and some new relationships with a very important client. My guess was John wanted to tell me, in person, that we hadn't won the work. In retrospect, that news wouldn't have been so bad...

At 9:00 a.m. John knocked on my door.

"Come on in John, even bad news might be welcome if it gives me a break from writing this damn attendance policy."

John came in, sat down, and looked awfully serious.

He started with a deep breath. "Andy, you know how much I've loved working here right?"

Uh oh.

"From day one, I've put my heart and soul into this job. I've worked crazy hours and never complained. I've prioritized this company over family and friends because I always felt we were doing something important for our clients and employees."

"What's your point, John?" I interrupted.

"I just don't feel it anymore Andy. I used to have so much passion for the work we did that I didn't care what it took to get the job done. Now I'm looking at my watch all day counting the hours and wishing I was somewhere else."

"I know business has been a little rough but we'll get back on track."

"You don't understand Andy. I can deal with things when they get rough. We've been through difficult times before and gotten through it. The problem is this place has changed. You've changed too."

"Now wait a minute John, I've got a business to run and could use some support. I'm sorry if I'm not a ray of sunshine everyday! You're out there wining and dining clients while I need to deal with real life back here. Do you know what it's like spending half your day putting out fires?"

"That's just my point Andy. It's not fun anymore. We always said, if it wasn't fun, we'd stop doing it."

I slumped back in my chair and waited for the other shoe to drop. And then he hit me with it...

PERFORMANCE BREAKTHROUGH

"Andy, I've decided to move on. Vincore offered to take me back with a promotion and it's too good an opportunity to pass up." He took a deep breath, "I'm giving you my two-week notice."

I was speechless. Although I owned the firm, I never thought of John as an employee, he was more of a partner. How could he do this to the company? How could he do this to me? For the lack of anything constructive to say, my reaction was short, sweet and pretty heartless.

"Thanks for everything John. No need for a two-week notice; you can leave as soon as you gather your personal belongings."

"Andy, please don't…"

"Goodbye John. I've got work to do."

Upon reflection, working on that attendance policy was the best part of my day.

* * *

A *QUADROPHENIA* KIND OF NIGHT

The drive home that night was a chance to unwind. Listening to motivational CD's or upbeat music would not do the trick. Instead, it was The Who's *Quadrophenia*—a rock opera about suicidal youth in 60s London…not exactly upbeat. Alone in the car, screaming every word to every angry, suicidal song changed my mood alright. I've always liked anger better than depression anyway.

I said it was a chance to unwind, I didn't say I actually unwound.

As I put my key in the door, I heard yelling coming from inside the house. Either my family was listening to *Quadrophenia* too, or my son had another banner day at school. Ah, home sweet home.

I was tempted to turn around and jump back in the car again but, against my better judgment, I went inside.

"Hello, I'm home!" I tried to scream over the yelling.

The yelling continued but I heard the pitter patter of six feet running down the stairs to greet me. My three-year-old Labrador retriever jumped me, and my ten-year-old daughter was not far behind.

"Hi Daddy! Wanna see my new dance routine?"

PERFORMANCE BREAKTHROUGH

"Sure honey, let's see."

Jenny was actually an excellent dancer. One of the highlights of my year was going to her dance recital. However, this show was interrupted by Rocky jumping all over her with each new move.

"You and Rocky make a great team honey. How was school?"

"Good, but I gotta go. I was in the middle of IM'ing my friends and they're probably wondering where I am."

She lives half her life on the computer. It's a wonder kids ever leave the house these days.

I walked into the kitchen to find my wife Susan and my twelve-year-old son Bobby in the heat of battle. This battle, like most, was caused by another rough day at school.

We found out a year earlier that Bobby had something called Asperger's syndrome. Asperger's is difficult to describe, but I think it was created to push my buttons and test the limits of my sanity.

It's basically a high-functioning form of autism. Although individual cases can be very different, people with Asperger's develop a very narrow and deep set of likes and interests as a way of blocking out the world because the world is too overwhelming for them.

Bobby's interests were T.V., video games and...did I mention video games. He had an obsession with his way of doing things and a very black and white way of looking at the world. Relating to people was very difficult for him. His lack of natural social skills and rigid set of interests gave him a maturity level much younger than his twelve years.

It wasn't all bad though; he also had an incredible memory, terrific math skills, and came out with some hilarious comments from time to time. Like the time he said a cemetery was "like a garden of dead people." Asperger's kids definitely have a different way of looking at the world.

It started when Bobby was about a year and a half. He was way behind in his ability to speak and had a temper so bad he had a black and blue mark on his forehead for six months from banging it against the wall and floor. Over the next nine years, he was diagnosed with almost every three-letter acronym I'd ever heard of. Issues ran from heartbreaking to frustrating.

For example, when he was nine Bobby spent two weeks putting his head inside his shirt and sitting in the hallway at school during lunch. The teachers tried to get him to go back into the lunchroom, but he wouldn't move or speak. It turns out the other kids were teasing him and that was his way of dealing with it. Fifth graders can be pretty cruel to someone who's "different." I know; I was one of those cruel fifth graders a long time ago.

Then, there's the issue of getting up in the morning and getting ready for school. If we didn't stay on top of him every step of the way—waking up, getting dressed, brushing his teeth, etc.—he would forget what he needed to do and sit down to pet the dog for twenty minutes. It was a constant struggle getting him out of the house on time.

He also didn't learn the way other children did. Most kids naturally picked up on social cues and basic life skills by watching others. Bobby needed to be taught these skills, usually unwillingly, every step of the way.

Like I said…heartbreaking and frustrating.

Anyway, back to the yelling I heard when I walked in. "What happened now?" For some unknown reason I decided to join the battle instead of tiptoeing away quietly.

"School is soooo boring! I can't stand it anymore! The other kids are annoying and the teachers treat me like I'm in jail!"

"I know all that," I complained. "You've been telling me that every day for the last six years, but what specifically happened today?"

That's when my wife jumped in. "Tell daddy what you said to your teacher."

"I don't remember," he lied.

"Bobby, I'll find out one way or another so you might as well tell me."

"Okay…I um, told Mrs. Mackay she was a moron."

"Excuse me?"

"She wouldn't leave me alone. She kept trying to get me to finish my writing assignment but I had nothing left to write. I hate writing!"

I won't bore you with the rest of the conversation but it ended with a bit more screaming and three Nintendo-less days for my son.

* * *

"What are we gonna do with him? Things seem to be getting worse," Susan said as we got into bed that evening.

"I don't know but, to be honest, I just can't deal with it now. I'm living a nightmare at work and things seem to be getting worse, not better. By the way, that new psychologist is really working miracles with Bobby," I said sarcastically.

About three months ago we started seeing our third family psychologist in the last two years. None of them seemed to have any more of a clue than Susan and I did about how to get through to Bobby. This last one said he'd worked with Asperger's kids. I guess I should have asked if he actually *helped* them as well.

"I plan on making some calls tomorrow. I got a recommendation from ASPEN that I'd like us to check out." ASPEN is an Asperger's support group we'd recently joined.

"Great," I said. Although all I was thinking was, "here we go again."

* * *

THE LEADERSHIP TEAM

The next morning it was time to tell the team John had quit. I'm sure most already knew, but I needed to make it official and get their thoughts. I scheduled a meeting of my leadership team for 9:00 a.m.

When I arrived at 7:15, the message light on my phone was on. That was never good news. For some reason, if someone left a message during the day it was fifty-fifty whether it would be good news or bad. But, when someone left a message over-night, it was almost always some problem that would screw up most of the next day. My prediction was right.

The message was from Vault Communications. A competitor had beaten us out for the new project we had proposed. They liked our ideas but just thought our team lacked the passion they needed to be successful. This was going to throw a major wrench in our ability to meet our sales forecast for the following quarter. In addition, since our current project with them was due to be completed at the end of that month; it also meant ten more people on the bench.

The worst part of the message was the passion comment. It was an eerie echo of John's complaint when he quit the day before. Was John right? Of course he was. Most of our employees looked like they were sleepwalking through the day. The question was why were they sleeping and how could I have woken them up?

PERFORMANCE BREAKTHROUGH

I decided to call Vault to see if there was any way to save the business and get another chance. No one was there so I left a voicemail. One I knew would probably not be returned.

Ah, another beautiful start to the day.

* * *

The team meeting didn't start until about 9:15 a.m. I was there promptly at 9 a.m., but the full team hadn't staggered in for another fifteen minutes. I guess when you're sleepwalking it's hard to find the conference room.

Now that John was gone, my leadership team was made up of four directors.

Kim Edwards headed up our consumer products industry group. She had been with us for a year and a half and made an impact from day one. She was incredibly bright and talented. Most clients loved Kim because she was as honest as they came. Some hated her for the same reason. If she felt strongly about something, you were going to hear it whether you liked it or not. Tact was not one of her finer qualities.

Joe Cialone headed up our utilities and telecommunications industry group. Joe was with us from the beginning. What Joe lacked in consulting skills, he made up for with his incredible network. He knew everyone and everyone knew him. If you needed a good plumber, Joe knew a guy. If you needed a great seat to a concert, Joe knew a guy. If you needed a contact at a potential client, Joe knew a guy.

THE LEADERSHIP TEAM

Rich Anderson headed up our technology services group. Rich's team was made up of "bits and bytes" techies that supported the work of the industry groups. He had been with us about two years but I don't think any of us really felt like we knew him. He did a solid job with our tech group. His team and our clients really respected him, but he liked to keep to himself more often than not.

Linda Friedman was our controller. Like Joe, Linda had been with us from day one. Nobody knew numbers like Linda. She had a photographic memory and could quote budget line items in her sleep. Linda was old school and ruled our numbers and her team with an iron fist.

"From the serious look on your faces, I'm sure you all know John resigned yesterday," I started. I decided not to say anything about the Vault Communications message yet.

The nods around the table were unanimous.

Kim chimed in first. "Tell me you didn't see that coming Andy."

"No Kim, I didn't. I always thought of John as a friend and a loyal member of the team. I know we've been going through a rough time but I didn't expect he'd quit on us."

"He didn't 'quit on us, Andy," Kim countered. "He left for what he thought was a better opportunity. I spoke to him yesterday before he left. He was pretty upset. He didn't want it to come to this but he did what he felt he had to do. We all see what's happened to the business over the last year and frankly, it's pretty scary."

"Come on Kim," Linda, visibly angry, entered the conversation. "If John made his sales numbers we wouldn't be in this situation in the first place. Seems to me we're better off without him."

"Now wait a minute Linda. None of us are happy about this situation, but we're not going to sit hear and disparage John," I quickly shifted gears in defense of my old friend. "He helped us build this company and I've considered him a friend for a long time. I'm angry too, but beating him up after he's walked out the door won't help the situation. We need to look forward and figure out how to deal with this."

"The more important issue," Joe agreed, "is what do we do now? Should we try to find a replacement, or just split up his responsibilities?"

"I disagree," Kim argued. "Our priority needs to be figuring out how to make sure the rest of us don't follow John out the door. How do we inject some passion back in to this place? How do we make this a rewarding place to work again?"

As usual, Kim was right on the money.

"I agree with Kim. We obviously need to fill in the gap for John's responsibilities, but our priority needs to be fixing the problems that lead to this. What do you think Linda?" I knew she'd have some strong opinions and wanted to bring her into the conversation.

"I'm honestly not sure I see the problem," Linda said with a confused look. "People leave companies all the time and you just need to deal with it. They're only loyal to themselves. You can't blame them. I don't feel like it's our job to make sure people are passionate about what they do," she said with a sarcastic accent on the word passionate. "They have a job to do and they should do it. They should be thankful they have a job. If it doesn't make them passionate, they should grow up or find something else."

"And you think we should just let people go without trying to do something about it?" Rich said, amazed at Linda's attitude.

"Here's what we're going to do," I interrupted before Linda had a chance to answer. "I want each of you to spend a significant amount of time over the next week speaking with your teams and doing some hard thinking yourselves about our situation. We need to understand why we're in this situation and how the heck to get out. I'd like to get back together in a week to talk about our challenges and brainstorm what we need to do about it. I need you all to take this assignment very seriously. In the meantime, I'll take over John's responsibilities."

"Sounds like a good idea Andy," Joe said smiling. "The only problem is, with you heading up business development, we may be out of business by next week."

At least someone still had a sense of humor.

* * *

TOUGH DECISIONS

"I really think this psychologist knows what he's talking about," Susan said after we put the kids to sleep. "I called two references and they loved him. He specializes in Asperger's and has some pretty unique ideas. He sounded real nice too."

"Okay, what's the next step?" I asked skeptically, as always.

"We need to make an appointment to go for an initial evaluation. There's only one problem. He's not on our insurance."

Oh great. "So what's it gonna cost us?"

"He charges 250 dollars per week."

"Susan, you know we can't afford that right now. We're barely getting by as it is, and my business line of credit just ran out. Isn't there someone on our insurance we can use?"

"Andy, you know we've tried that and have never found anyone that was any good. If this is a chance to help Bobby, we've got to find a way!"

I sat down and put my head in my hands.

"I've got an idea, but you won't like it," she said.

I looked up and waited.

"Brad from Vincore has been calling you every week to…"

"No way!" I interrupted. "I'm not going back there. You know how much this business means to me. For the first time in my life I have a company that's mine. I can't give up and I won't go back to Vincore with my tail between my legs."

"I hate to put it to you this way Andy, but what's more important, your son or your business?"

"That's not fair Susan. You know there's nothing I want more than for Bobby to live a normal life. And nothing I want more for us."

"So what do we do?"

"Make the appointment," I said. "We'll find a way to pay for it."

* * *

IDENTIFYING THE ISSUES

A week later it was time for our leadership team meeting. I was hopeful the directors had some productive discussions with their teams.

The meeting was scheduled to start at 9:00 a.m. and everyone was there on time except for Linda. We waited about five minutes and then decided to get started anyway.

"Thanks for your efforts this week guys. I'm sure it wasn't easy preparing for this meeting and still getting your jobs done." I stood up and walked over to the flip chart.

I knew I could count on Kim to get the ball rolling. She was the strongest member of my leadership team and wouldn't hesitate to be honest about our issues. She sometimes lacked tact, but that's not what we needed right now.

"Kim, let's get started with you; what'd you find?"

"I had one-on-one meetings with each of my team members and a full team meeting yesterday. The meetings were productive but, I've got to be honest," she hesitated, "the information I gathered was pretty depressing. Once I got the team to open up, they had a lot to say.

"First, and not unexpected, they all feel like they're kept in the dark as to what's going on around here. They figure if we're keeping secrets, things must be pretty bad, which makes them feel like their jobs are in jeopardy."

I wrote "Fear/Lack of job security" on our flip chart.

"Second, they don't seem to know what's expected of them. They understand we have monthly sales and profit goals, but have no idea what their role is in helping us meet those goals."

I added "Unclear expectations/goals" to the chart.
"And third, and most disturbing, they don't seem to be motivated by what we do. They have an 'it's just a job' type attitude. I tried to push them to tell me what pumped them up about the work and I got blank stares."

When she was done, I summarized her points on the flip chart as:

1. Fear/Lack of job security
2. Unclear expectations/goals
3. No passion

"I think this list probably sums it up Kim. Did they have anything positive to say?" I asked.

"They liked the sandwiches I brought to the meeting," she said with a big sarcastic smile.

Looks like I'd be listening to *Quadrophenia* on the way home again.

IDENTIFYING THE ISSUES

As I was about to move on, Linda walked in and sat down. I was unhappy she was late to the meeting but I decided to ignore it and move on. "Joe, why don't you go next."

Joe gave his report, and Rich after him. They had both spent a significant amount of time meeting with their teams as well. Although the information was depressing, I was very impressed by their efforts.

By the time we got to Linda, the flipchart was getting full.

1. Fear/Lack of job security
2. Unclear expectations/goals
3. No passion
4. Lack of freedom to get the work done
5. Work is too serious—no fun
6. Lack of interesting learning opportunities
7. Not enough performance feedback

"Linda, how'd you do with your team this week?"

"I'm sorry guys; we had a bunch of fires to put out and didn't have the time to get together. Looks like you all put together a great list though. I'm sure my team would share the same thoughts," she said, looking down at her notepad and seeming uninterested.

"Linda, you do realize how important this is, right?" I said, frustrated.

"Come on Andy, are you serious? How is all of this going to help? We have a job to get done and, if my team wants to keep their jobs, they better do it. Talking about their *feelings,"*—she said 'feelings' like it was a dirty word—"is a waste of time. If they want to feel something, they should feel lucky to have a job."

The silence was deafening for before Joe came to the rescue.

"You're living in the past Linda," Joe said angrily. "People don't just feel lucky to have a job anymore; they want some fulfillment in their work. This is a different world than it was thirty years ago when people expected to work for one company their whole lives. And it works both ways; company loyalty and employee loyalty are things of the past. If we don't focus on ways to motivate our staff and keep them happy, someone else will."

"Excellent point, Joe," Rich chimed in. "We obviously have a pretty serious problem here. We can't make it go away by wishing people had a stronger work ethic."

I was about to interject, but I decided to sit back and listen. While I was very disappointed in Linda's attitude, I was happy to finally see some passion coming from the team again. I was also proud of Rich and Joe for sticking up for what they thought was right. I needed the team to own the problem and, eventually, the solution. So I decided to let the conversation get a bit more heated before stepping in.

Not unexpectedly, Kim joined the fray.

"Linda, it seems to me you're the only one of us who didn't spend time speaking with your team about our situation this week. If you did speak with them, what do you think they would have said?"

"I'm sure they're not too happy. Look how our numbers are trending. Who would be happy?"

"Don't you think it would be helpful to speak with them about it…to better understand their concerns?" Kim pushed.

"I think the best way to deal with their concerns," Linda said, now getting a bit red in the face, "is to make sure they know they've got to start working harder or they may not have a job to be concerned about. You'll see. It'll be amazing how morale improves once our numbers improve."

Now I decided to interject. "The question is *will* our numbers improve without first fixing our morale problem? I, for one, am not willing to make that bet. We've got a good list of our problems, but now we need to focus on some solutions. For now, I'd like to meet this time every week to brainstorm ideas. Don't be afraid to use your team as a sounding board. I want you all to understand this is our highest priority project so I'll expect your commitment and your best efforts." I looked around to make sure the team was on board. All nodded, except for Linda who just stared straight ahead.

"Thanks everyone. Linda I'd like you to stick around for a few minutes so we can talk."

Kim, Rich, and Joe filed out, while Linda stayed behind. She was rolling her eyes, visibly frustrated.

"Linda, why were you late to the meeting?"

PERFORMANCE BREAKTHROUGH

"I told you, we had some fires to put out. Your choice Andy; what's more important: making sure there are no mistakes in our monthly numbers, or getting to a meeting on time?"

"You don't seem to understand that unless we solve our people problems, there will be no monthly numbers. Linda, I need to know you're with me on this."

She took a deep breath. "I'm with you Andy. I'll be on time next week."

I waited for something more. Something to give me some confidence we were on the same page.

"Can I go now?" was all she added.

"Sure, thanks Linda."

Linda was a problem I was going to have to deal with sooner or later.

* * *

HOLD ON!

"Honey, can you get Bobby off of Nintendo," Susan yelled from upstairs. "We've got to leave in fifteen minutes."

It was time to see psychologist number four. I had long ago stopped thinking that there'd be some magic answer to Bobby's Asperger's issues, but I still held out hope that a competent therapist would help add some sanity to our lives.

"Bobby, it's time to get off Nintendo!" I yelled into the den (in my house, we yelled all the time), where Bobby was mesmerized by strange characters running, jumping, and killing God knows what.

"Hold on, I need to finish this level!"

"No, you don't! Shut it off and go get ready. We have to leave!" This exact conversation happens about twice a day. I should just tape myself saying this and time it to go off every six hours or so. Sometimes I feel like if I hear Bobby say "hold on" one more time, my head will explode.

"Why do I need to go?" Jenny whined from her room. "I'm not the one with Appleberger's or whatever it's called."

"Because you can't stay home by yourself. And besides, this is a family therapist. That means his job is to try to help all of us. Bobby, are you off Nintendo yet?"

PERFORMANCE BREAKTHROUGH

"Hold on, I'm almost done!"

No...head hasn't exploded yet.

Here's the part where I walk into the den and threaten him with a fate worse than death. "Bobby, shut that off now or I'll shut it and you'll lose Nintendo for a week," I said as I stormed into the den.

Surprisingly, we made it to the therapist with no heads exploding and no lost Nintendo time. Sometimes miracles do happen.

* * *

DR. MOSS AND THE FIRST SECRET

I guess miracles come in pairs. Our new therapist, Dr. Moss, actually had some interesting ideas we hadn't heard two hundred times before.

"Over the first four therapy sessions," Dr. Moss began, "I will be sharing four secrets with you that will change your lives in more ways than you can imagine."

It all sounded very mysterious and he had us hooked. We all leaned forward in our seats to hear what this interesting character was going to say next.

"These secrets," he continued, "are guaranteed to work. However, you must promise to implement each secret during the week following our session. In the next session, you will share your experiences trying to implement the secret and how it's changed your life. We will then discuss the next secret."

Who was this guy and what planet was he from?

We then discussed the first secret. It was called *acceptance*. This meant accepting Bobby for who he was instead of who we wanted him to be. For years, we had been trying to make Bobby normal in his problem areas instead of understanding what made him unique, and loving him unconditionally. We needed to start seeing the world through Bobby's eyes instead of our own. He had some significant challenges and they weren't going to go away by us telling him to work harder. We needed to have a more empathetic mindset, which meant we needed to appreciate and validate his point of view. It also meant we needed to stop thinking we needed to treat him like any other typical kid. He wasn't typical…and that was okay.

It wasn't about changing Bobby…it was about changing ourselves. It was about changing how we viewed him. It was about changing our expectations of him and how we reacted to him.

This wasn't a magic bullet, and there was no miracle. However, this simple concept did have an impact on our home environment over the next few days. Just accepting that Bobby had different motivations, ways of learning, and ways of communicating significantly decreased the constant yelling. It didn't cure his Asperger's—there is no cure, only management of the disorder—but it helped us start to create a more supportive environment. As parents, we were trying to shift Bobby's view of us from jail wardens to problem solvers.

We knew this wouldn't solve our problems overnight and there were many other things for us to learn. But after years of frustration, it was a pretty good start.

* * *

THE END-GAME

During the week since our last team leadership meeting, things hadn't improved. We had no luck winning back the Vault Communications project and that didn't help morale any. We needed to get our act together quickly or we'd see more resignations and more red ink.

The time came for our first weekly brainstorming session and Kim, Joe, Rich, and Linda were all there on time. That was a good start.

I had taped the flip chart from the past week's meeting on the wall as a reminder of our issues:

1. Fear/Lack of job security
2. Unclear expectations/goals
3. No passion
4. Lack of freedom to get the work done
5. Work is too serious—no fun
6. Lack of interesting learning opportunities
7. Not enough performance feedback

"Well, now that we know how screwed up we are, we need to figure out what we're going to do about it." I said to the group, referring to the flip chart. "However, instead of starting with potential solutions, I'd like to start with the end-game. In other words, we know what our employees are saying about A.M.

PERFORMANCE BREAKTHROUGH

Consulting today; what do we want them to be saying six months from now?"

"It seems to me we want the opposite of what they're saying today," Rich recommended.

"You may be right Rich," I answered, "but I'm not sure it's that simple. I think discussing our vision of a more positive work environment may help us to determine some priorities, and maybe some solutions. We may not think it's important to solve every one of the problems on the list. On the other hand, we may come up with some things we'd like to improve that didn't even make the list. I don't want to jump to any quick solutions. The decisions we make in these brainstorming meetings need to guide us back to health. It's critical that we think this through. We may not get a second chance."

There was silence for a minute or two while I let the group think about this new question.

Joe started the ball rolling. "I think we want this to be a place where people can grow; a place where people can reach their potential."

"Great start Joe; give me a bit more detail."

"The only way we can become an extraordinary company is to have extraordinary people. The only way to do that is to help them reach their potential. Remember, our employees have other options. If they are not growing here, they'll choose to grow somewhere else."

"How is this different from what we're doing today?" Kim challenged. "We train our people and we pay them fairly...what are you saying we should do differently?"

"I think it's a difference in focus," Joe explained. "We've always focused on the company's goals. Now I'm not saying that's wrong, but what about our employees' goals? Do any of us know what's important to them beyond a paycheck? If we can do some things to help them achieve their goals, don't you think they might be more passionate about this place?"

"That sounds like a nice concept, but I'm not sure we have the time to do our own jobs, let alone helping our people with their personal goals," Linda answered.

This time, Rich jumped in. "I disagree Linda. All we're talking about is having a better understanding of our employees' career goals and the areas they'd like to develop further. To me it seems like a fair trade. If our employees are willing to help the company grow, we ought to be willing to help them grow as well. Too many good people have left this company over the last year. Don't you think some of them would have stayed if they felt like we cared as much about them as the bottom line?"

"I know it sounds kind of hokey, but I love it," Kim slapped her hand on the table for emphasis. "We strengthen our team and improve employee loyalty at the same time."

Everyone else seemed to agree as well, so I added "Foster growth/reach potential" to a new flip chart page.

Rich was next. "I think we need our employees to feel some ownership for what we do. They need to feel like they have some impact, that they're not just cogs in a big machine."

"How do we do that?" Linda asked skeptically.

"Let's not worry about how we're going to get there yet," I interjected. "Let's just focus on the destination. The question is do we think it would be beneficial for our people to feel more ownership in the company?"

"Of course it would," Joe answered. "Sometimes I think my team is paralyzed if I'm not there to make a decision for them. It would make my life much easier if they felt like they had the freedom to make decisions that had some real impact."

Again they were unanimous nods around the table, so I added "Ownership/Impact" to the flipchart.

"What else guys? I think we're on a nice roll…let's keep going."

"How about setting clear expectations?" Kim offered. "People can't take ownership for making decisions if they don't know where we're headed and what's expected of them. They also need to be real clear about their role in achieving our goals."

I was skeptical. "I'm not sure what you mean Kim. I've sent a ton of memos and emails about our revenue and profit goals. In fact, we discussed our actual numbers versus our plan at the town hall meeting last month."

"That's fine at the company level, but do our people really understand how their jobs contribute to the whole? I'm not sure we're all real clear on how our performance as a team or as an individual relates to the company's goals. If we had more clarity around team and individual goals, the actions we need to take might be much clearer."

After another round of nods, I added "Clear Expectations" to the flip chart.

"These are all great ideas, but how about making sure we have a little fun around here too?" Joe asked as he floated a paper airplane across the room. "We need to laugh more, play more, and make sure people feel rewarded for the work they do. It can't be all work and no play, right?"

Linda had enough of this. "What are we talking about guys? We're worried that our employees aren't having fun? This isn't a party; we've got a business to run. I'm all for improvement, but I don't think we get there by treating our employees like children. I've got real work to do."

With that, Linda got up and stormed out of the meeting. The rest of us stared in complete shock before I broke the awkward silence.

"Well, that was interesting. Believe it or not, I think Linda just helped us with our next item on the list. I may not agree with her point of view, but her passion is something I wish more of us had. John said it when he resigned. He said he didn't feel the passion anymore and, you know what, I don't think any of us have felt it for a long time. Our mission should be to get that passion back."

With that, I added our last two points to the flip chart and put it side by side with our list of issues.

Where We Are Now	Where We Want To Be
• Fear/Lack of job security • Unclear expectations/goals • No passion • Lack of freedom • Too serious – no fun • Lack of interesting learning opportunities • Not enough performance feedback	• Foster Growth/Reach Potential • Ownership/Impact • Clear Expectations • Fun & Rewarding • Passion

With everyone, except Linda, in agreement, we now had our vision. I had two immediate next steps. First, I needed to deal with the "Linda situation." Second, I needed to get ready for the following week's brainstorming where we'd start figuring out how to reach our new vision. Luckily, I had an interesting thought as to how we might get started.

* * *

LINDA

Linda was waiting for me in my office when I got back after the meeting.

I was ready for typical Linda—gruff, no-nonsense, and pissed off at my overly-sensitive attitude towards our staff. I'd had enough and was ready to end it right there. She was a problem, and a potential cancer within our organization, that had to be dealt with.

I started to speak and Linda interrupted. "Andy, if you want me to resign, I totally understand." Her voice sounded shaky, like she could cry at any moment. I'd never heard her like that. I was in shock.

"Linda, what's going on?"

"Andy, I'm not sure I can do this. I've spent thirty years of my life doing things one way. People didn't always love me, but that was okay. I got the job done and got it done well. That was always enough." She stared into space for a few seconds. "Maybe the world has passed me by."

"Linda you know you were always an important part of our success and I'd love for you to be an important part of our turn-around. I'm not asking you to change who you are; I'm only asking that you do your best to support the changes we're trying to make around here. I don't expect you to shift from ruling with an iron fist to being a cheerleader, but I do expect your support. Your attitude lately is hurting, not helping."

"I don't know Andy. You guys may be better off without me. You want the truth? I didn't speak with my team last week because I was afraid of what they'd say. I have no idea if they like working for me because I never thought that stuff was important. I know numbers better than anyone else. It's what I do; it's what I've always done. Motivating people has never been my strength and I know that's what we need right now." She looked down at the ground and I could tell she was trying to hold back the tears.

With all of Linda's challenges, I still wasn't sure I wanted to lose her. I needed to give her some hope and boost her confidence a bit.

"Linda, we need a lot of things right now, not just motivational skills. You've got analytical abilities like no one else I've ever seen. You've got more experience in this business than anyone else in the company. And you've got an unbelievable work ethic and passion for this company. I'd say those are some critical talents we can't afford to lose around here."

"Wow, you make me sound pretty good." I almost detected a slight smile.

"I can't say I know where we're headed on this journey of ours, but I know we've got some real challenges ahead of us. Our organization may look very different before we're done, so I can't make any promises. All I can say is that I could really use your support right now. I'll be honest though, if you're going to stay,

LINDA

I need you squarely on the team; not fighting us. Do you think you can do that?"

"Well you know I'll always challenge the team, but I'll try to make sure to do it in a productive way."

"No more blowing off assignments or walking out of meetings?" I asked.

"Deal, Andy."

"Welcome back, Linda."

* * *

ACCEPTANCE

Another week passed and it was time for the next brainstorming session.

"I've been doing a great deal of thinking over the last week about what we need to do to start attacking our problems," I began. "You all know that my son Bobby has Asperger's syndrome, right?" There were confused nods around the table as they wondered where I was going with this. "Well, I think his new therapist may have given me an idea that may help us."

Joe was perplexed. "You talked to your therapist about our issues at work?"

"Are you gonna take away our Nintendo time"? Rich whined.

"Very funny guys. His name is Dr. Moss and he recommended something to help the situation with Bobby, and believe it or not, I think it just might be a great first step for us as a business as well. He's teaching us these four secrets, and the first one is called *acceptance*. It means accepting someone for who they are instead of who you want them to be. Let me ask you all a question: you've all heard of the golden rule, right?" They nodded. "Well do you agree with it?"

"Of course," Kim answered. "Treat others the way you would want to be treated; who wouldn't agree with that?"

"Really?" I responded sarcastically. "Then you believe we're all exactly the same?"

"Well…no," Kim hesitated, realizing where I was going.

"If we're all different, why do we think everyone wants to be treated the way *we'd* want to be treated? Shouldn't we treat them the way *they* want to be treated?"

"Fair point Andy, but how does this impact our business," Linda asked, still a bit confused.

"Each one of our employees has goals, motivations, values, and learning styles. By understanding and acting on these differences, we should be able to get a lot more out of our team.

"For example, some of us are motivated by money, some by status, and others by free-time and flexibility. Should we offer the same types of incentives to all of them? Of course not."

Seeing slow agreement with my point, I added another example. "How about learning? Some employees learn best by studying everything there is to know about a task before trying it. Forcing them to begin a task before they're ready would result in poor execution and diminished confidence. Other employees like to learn by doing. They like to understand the basics of the task and then be let loose to learn from their mistakes. Studying the details of a task for too long would only bore them and de-motivate them. Would you train these different types of employees the same way? I hope not."

ACCEPTANCE

"Wait a minute Andy," Rich challenged, "treating everyone different worries me. Don't we need to treat everyone the same... isn't that what's fair?"

"I know treating everyone the same is management 101 Rich, but do we do that because it's fair or because it's easy?" I asked, not expecting an answer. "I think we learn to manage that way because it's easy...not because it's right."

"That makes a lot of sense, Andy. It seems to me the key is knowing our employees well enough to act on their differences," added Kim.

"Exactly," I agreed. "The sad thing is that most of us don't know our teams well enough to understand these differences, and that includes me! I hate to admit it, but I'm not sure I know you guys anywhere near as well as I should."

"So how do we get to know these things about our employees?" Rich asked, sounding eager to put this into action. "If you asked me to tell you what motivates me most or how I learn best, I'm not sure I'd be able to give you a real accurate answer. I'm honestly not sure I know myself that well. And, even if I did, I might decide to tell you what I thought you wanted to hear, as opposed to the truth, which might not be so impressive."

"Great point Rich. There are probably some more creative ways we could ask those types of questions," I answered. "What if we asked them what they like and dislike about the job? Or to tell us about a time they were incredibly motivated at work and then ask them why they felt that way? We could also ask them to remember a time they learned something new very quickly. Then ask them how they learned it. Not only will you find out an incredible amount of useful information, you'll also show them how much you care. We can also watch them. How do they act in meetings? Do they take the lead or do they sit back and play devil's advocate? How do they seem to learn best? What type of recognition seems to motivate them most?"

"I would also think personality assessments could help," Kim chimed in.

"I was on a team once where the manager made sure they had a 'personal history' discussion with each employee. She asked about their life growing up, favorite hobbies, family, etc. I think this really helped her understand what made people tick," added Joe.

"Those are great suggestions guys," I offered, feeling great about their input and enthusiasm.

"But what do we do differently once we know these things," Joe asked.

"Great question, Joe. If we get to know our employees better but still do things the same old ways, we haven't achieved anything," I added. "Any thoughts?"

"I think we should look at our training programs and make sure we can adapt them to better support different learning styles," Kim offered.

ACCEPTANCE

"We should also look at our compensation structure to make sure our incentives can be flexed to motivate people in different ways," Joe added. "That ought to help us with recruiting as well. We may even want to look at some flex-time ideas for our employees at different stages of their lives. This might help us with working moms or our more senior employees.

"And what about giving some of our folks the option of getting involved in some community service projects?" asked Kim. "I know I've got some people on my team that are really into that sort of thing."

"This is a terrific start guys," I complimented the group. "I'll put together a summary of these thoughts with some division of responsibilities for diving into these ideas in more detail. This is only the first step and I'm sure we have a lot more brainstorming to do before we come up with ways to solve all of our problems. We'll get back together next week to review how we're doing and brainstorm some additional ideas. In the meantime, you should be using the ideas we discussed to speak with your individual team members to get to know them better. As a first step, I'll be scheduling meetings with all of you to do the same."

I was excited about our future for the first time in a long time. I knew we had a long way to go, but I felt like we were headed in the right direction. The company results hadn't changed, but I felt like we were starting to tackle some of the issues that were holding us back from our potential.

* * *

ACCEPTANCE SUMMARY

The first step is to accept that we're all different.

Do you adhere to the adage that all employees should be treated equally? If so, our employees will never achieve their true potential, and never be truly happy in their work.

Each one of your employees has different goals, motivations, values, and learning styles. By understanding and acting on these differences you will be able to bring the best out of your team.

Forget the golden rule, which states, "Treat others as **you** would want to be treated," and replace it with the platinum rule, which states, "Treat others as **they** would want to be treated."

"Starter" Ideas:

☑ **Dig deep**
Get beyond the superficial and learn about your employees and what makes them tick. Take advantage of the following ways to dig deep:

☑ <u>Conduct personal histories meetings/ discussions</u> – Find out about your employees' childhood, families, hobbies, favorite jobs, etc. These meetings can happen one-on-one or in groups.

☑ <u>Ask</u> – Meet one-on-one with each team member to ask them about their values, motivations, and learning styles. Here are some sample questions:

- Think back to a time when you were incredibly motivated at work. What happened right before that to make you feel that way?
- Think back to a time when you had to learn something new and it just "clicked" for you. What method of learning did you use?

☑ <u>Conduct personality assessments</u> – There are many good personality assessments on the market (Innermetrix, Profiles International, DISC, etc.). These assessments are typically very accurate and may give you, and your employees, important insight on their styles, talents, values and motivations.

☑ <u>Observe</u> – Watch your team during meetings, high stress situations, and social situations, and take note of their styles and reactions. Do they take the lead in meetings or do they follow? Are they agreeable or do they play devil's advocate? Do they thrive under pressure or wilt?

☑ **Understand generational dynamics**

The baby boomers think generation Y expects everything handed to them on a silver platter and can't understand their work ethic. Generation Y are incredibly tech savvy and multitask like no other generation has before. Generation X is caught in the middle of baby boomers who haven't retired yet, and don't want to anytime soon, and generation Y "kids" who are trying to leapfrog over them in the organization.

Each generation has value to add, as well as shortcomings. The trick is to understand that everyone is trying to do the best they can with a different set of values. As a leader, treating all generations the same can lead to disastrous results. Understanding and accepting generational differences will improve recruiting, retention, and productivity.

☑ **Differentiated learning and development**
One size DOES NOT fit all in the area of learning and development. Learning programs should incorporate a level of flexibility to support individuals with different needs and learning styles.

Some specific ways to add individual flexibility include:

o Self assessments to determine specific developmental needs
o Goal plans to tailor development action items
o Facilitated discussions to engage the audience instead of one-size-fits-all lectures
o Use of various delivery mechanisms including eLearning, instructor-led classes, webcasts, case studies, projects, activities, and workshops

☑ **Differentiated motivation/compensation**
We tend to try to motivate people the way *we* would
be motivated. We assume if we're motivated by money,
other people will be as well. The key here again is to incorporate a level of flexibility to support people in different life situations with different motivations.

If someone's primary motivation is quality time with
their family, incenting them with a dollar bonus if they
work extra hours will not work very well. Incenting
them with additional vacation time would be a much
better idea.

Instead of assuming that all bonuses and rewards
should be monetary, try some of these other incentives
depending on the motivations of the individual:

- o Vacation time
- o Time for volunteer work or other special interests
- o Donations to their favorite charity
- o Public recognition (town hall meeting, company
    newsletter, etc.)
- o Take them and their families out to dinner
- o Send them on a trip
- o Pay for training or a seminar they're interested in

☑ **Vary communication mediums**
Twenty years ago, communication was much simpler.
Face-to-face, phone, and print were just about the only
options we had. These days we've got email, instant
messaging, texting, webcasts, blogs, social networks,

and more. Choosing the right communication medium is more important than ever.

While generational differences aren't the only reason to vary communication mediums, it's certainly an important one. For an importance message, baby boomers may be much more responsive to face-to-face or phone communications. Generation Y may be just as comfortable with instant messaging or texting. You'll also find that while some people may never answer their phones, they'll respond to email with lightening speed. Others may only look at email once per day.

Before you communicate, make sure you understand the different communication styles within, and across teams, and vary communication mediums as necessary.

☑ **Flexible schedules**
The days of the nine-to-five husband and the stay-at-home housewife are obviously long gone. The days of working only while we're at the office are long gone too. Thanks to the internet and smart phones, we're able to work whenever and wherever we are.

This means that organizations should take advantage of flexible schedules for their employees. This is a major opportunity for improving employee retention and productivity.

* * *

THE SECOND SECRET

It was time for our next session with Dr. Moss. Given my new-found respect for him, I was actually looking forward to it. Not only did his acceptance idea help with my last brainstorming meeting with the team, we'd also been getting along better with Bobby. His Asperger's behaviors were obviously still there, but there were less shouting matches and he seemed a bit happier, as did the rest of the family. Although he would have never described it this way, I think he finally felt like he was getting some respect from the family. Maybe he was right.

During the session, we discussed some of the wins we had from the week before. We all congratulated ourselves for a job well done. Dr. Moss also introduced a new secret; he called this one *leverage*.

He explained that most parents spent 80 percent of their time negatively focused (finding what their kids were doing wrong and nagging them about it) and 20 percent of the time positively focused (encouraging their kids about the things they did well). In the case of an Asperger's kid like Bobby, it was probably closer to 95 percent negative and 5 percent positive. The effect this had on his self-esteem must have been devastating.

He then focused our discussion on identifying the things Bobby excelled at. This was a great discussion for us since Bobby, like most Asperger's kids, became hyper-focused on certain activities, resulting in some real strong skills in those areas. In

PERFORMANCE BREAKTHROUGH

Bobby's case, it was math, computer games, and his incredible memory.

This is where the idea of *leverage* came into play. Once we understood where Bobby excelled, we needed to leverage those skills by helping him continue to build them and better focus on how to use them productively. Logically, the results of this would be twofold: one, he would be much happier and motivated since he'd be able to focus more of his time in areas he enjoyed; and two, he'd have a better chance of becoming incredibly skilled in those areas. Both of these results would have major implications for Bobby throughout his life.

While I loved the idea of *leverage*, it wasn't a magic bullet. Bobby still had some destructive behaviors that we couldn't simply ignore. However, I thought focusing more of our attention on the positive things he was doing would be a great next step in our journey.

I also thought I knew what the topic would be for our next brainstorming session at work.

* * *

LEVERAGE

At our next leadership brainstorming meeting, I was eager to discuss how people had used *acceptance*. I was also eager to introduce the next secret.

I started, "How did it go with your teams this week?"

As usual, Kim was the first to jump in. "I met with my team last week right after our leadership meeting. I introduced the idea of *acceptance* and, I've got to admit, I'm not sure it went very well."

"What happened," I asked, a bit surprised.

"Well, I met with each of my direct reports individually and had some pretty insightful discussions. It was kind of depressing to find out how much I didn't know about what made my team tick. So, for me, that part of the discussion was really helpful. The difficult part was answering questions about how things would change based on this information. For example, now that I know Tracy is more motivated by time off with her family than money, what do I do about it? I mean, we've got a pretty strict attendance and time off policy. Can I change it just for her?"

"I had the same problem," Joe chimed in. "It's nice to know more about our employees, but it seems the real work is in changing our policies and procedures. Since we haven't made any of those changes yet, I'm afraid we may be frustrating people even more by having these discussions."

"I know this isn't easy guys but we need to have faith that we're on the right track. We can't change overnight but we need to let our teams know we care and give them the confidence that we're making progress. After today's meeting I'll identify some steering committees to look at things like our compensation structure, training, and work schedule policies so we can make some of the hard decisions we need to make and initiate some real change. Don't get discouraged. We're not going to turn A.M. Consulting around overnight. *Acceptance* was only the first step. We've got a lot more work to do."

"Uh oh, it sounds like you spoke to your son's therapist again," Rich said sarcastically.

"Well, as a matter of fact...I'd like to discuss the second secret, *leverage*."

"Let me ask a question." I continued, "If you were going out to celebrate with your team tonight, would you take them to a nice restaurant or a diner?"

They all gave me a confused look.

"What the heck are we celebrating?" Linda asked.

"It's hypothetical Linda. But, really, where would you go?"

Joe decided to play along. "Depends who's paying, but if it's on you, I'd go to a nice restaurant."

"Why is that?"

"Better food, nicer atmosphere, and I'd get to spend more of your money."

"Be careful how you spend our budget," Linda laughed. It was nice to see her playing along.

"Wait a minute; diners have menus about an inch thick," I interrupted. "You can get anything…a hamburger, crab cakes, a tuna sandwich, or a giant chocolate chip cookie. Wouldn't you rather go there than a restaurant that doesn't nearly have that number of choices?"

"They may have a lot of choices but none of them taste very good. Even though the restaurant might have a much slimmer selection, if you pick the right one you can get some great food," Kim countered.

"Oh I get it. You'd choose the place that was extraordinary at a few things versus the place with the well-rounded menu," I offered, hoping they'd get the message.

"You see, I think we all try to make diners out of our employees. We focus so much time on making sure they're *competent* in all areas of our business that we forget to spend time focusing in their areas of greatest strength."

I saw confused looks again so I continued.

"Okay, let me ask you another question: how many of you think it's important for your employees to be well-rounded?"

They all raised their hands.

"Really?" I said, feigning surprise. "I'm not sure I want well-rounded employees, but I do want a well-rounded team.

"The term well-rounded has always had a positive connotation, but I'm not sure that's what we should strive for. I'd rather have an employee that was extraordinary at a few things than mediocre in a whole bunch. Here's an example..." I drew the chart below on our flipchart.

Employee Performance

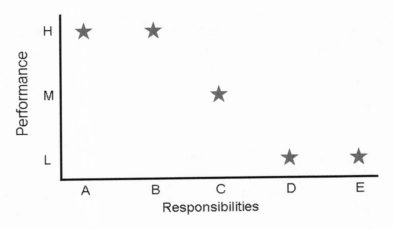

"Let's say you have a member of your team that's worked for you for about six months. So you know them well enough to understand their strengths and weaknesses, but haven't had enough time to really coach and mentor them.

LEVERAGE

"They perform at a very high level for two of their responsibilities." I pointed to the stars above responsibilities A and B on the chart. "They perform at a mediocre level for a third." I pointed to the star above responsibility C. "And low for the last two responsibilities." I pointed to the stars above responsibilities D and E.

"As a manager, where would you tend to spend most of your time?"

No one answered at first, so I prodded them a bit. "Put it this way, if one of your kids came home with two As, a B, and D on their report card, where would you focus first?"

"I'd probably focus on the D," Joe responded.

"So would it be any different for your employee?" I asked.

Joe hesitated at first, but answered, "I guess not. I'd probably want to spend a lot of time trying to fix their weakness."

"As would most of us, Joe," I continued. "But, let me ask you this, by focusing a great deal of time on the low performing responsibilities, do you think this person will become high performing in those areas?"

"No," Linda offered. "I'd probably get them close to mediocre, but in all likelihood they'd never become a star in those areas."

I circled the two low performing stars and drew an arrow that approached the mediocre level.

"Okay, and what do you think happens to the two high performing areas while you're spending so much time trying to
strengthen their weaknesses?"

"They'd probably start to dip a bit if we're not focusing on it and
their not getting reinforcement for their great work," Rich answered.

I then circled the two high performing stars and drew an arrow
approaching the mediocre level, resulting in the chart below.

Employee Performance

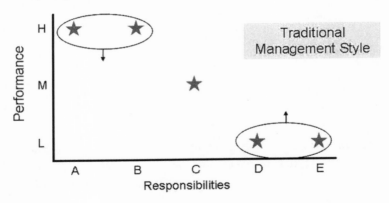

"Okay then. Using the traditional management philosophy of
spending most of our time working on weaknesses, where do
we end up?"

I drew a big circle around the resulting stars.

Employee Performance

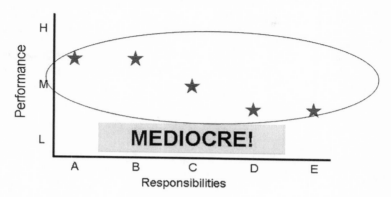

"With a mediocre employee," they all said in unison.

"How can we become a great company if our goal isn't to make our people great? If we want to have a remarkable company, we need remarkable people. Being well-rounded is not remarkable.

'We feel like our job is to identify our employee's weaknesses and try to fix them. What about their strengths? We barely pay attention to them. The result of this focus, at best, is an employee who can do most things but is not remarkable at anything. Sound familiar?"

The group seemed to be catching on so I continued my brief lecture.

"I think we've all seen that employees rarely become strong in an area of weakness. The best we can hope for is that they will rise to become mediocre. However, where an employee has talent, they can become world-class. In addition, focusing on maximizing those areas where they have true talent is incredibly motivating for them. Our job then becomes figuring out how to best *leverage* each employee's strengths to make them, and our company, great. Our job also needs to be building teams that include individuals that have all the strengths we need. We need well-rounded teams instead of well-rounded individuals."

"But we can't just ignore people's weaknesses," Joe challenged.

"I'm not suggesting we ignore weaknesses. By all means, if a weakness is getting in the way of doing the job, we need to find ways to manage it or compensate for it. We need to look for ways to get them to acceptable levels of performance, change their responsibilities, or let them go. But don't expect them to become experts tomorrow in those areas they're weak in today."

"I'm still not sure I get it Andy," Kim spoke for the group. "Maybe it would help if you gave some specific examples of strengths and weaknesses."

I had done some research and some thinking about this before the meeting so I described my thinking in some detail.

I started by describing strengths. Strengths were areas where employees just seemed to have raw talent or an innate ability in a specific area. These abilities probably began to emerge at a very young age, maybe six or seven. As an example, from a very young age, a child may exhibit strong leadership tendencies. With zero skills or experience, they somehow seem to take the lead in any group they're a part of. They just seem to have a knack for getting people to follow them anywhere. Other examples would include things like empathy, persuasiveness, competitiveness, assertiveness, or focus. They're also usually areas people feel incredibly passionate about.

The emergence of these talents is caused by the way our brains develop very early in life. Once our brains mature, it is very difficult, and sometimes impossible, to build a talent where one did not already exist. However, it is relatively easy to strengthen a talent that already exists.

I then described weaknesses. Weaknesses were not areas where employees performed poorly due to a lack of training or experience. They were areas where an employee seemed to have a low level of talent, regardless of the amount of effort they put in to build their skills. For example, trying to teach someone to be a better cold-caller, if they don't have a talent for persuasiveness, will be an uphill battle. No matter how many great cold-calling or closing techniques you teach them, they'll dread selling and probably never become much good.

If the weakness is knowledge-based (due to a lack of experience), the action plan would be to provide additional training and, potentially, allow more time for on-the-job experience.

We discussed three ways to deal with a talent-based weakness:

1. Partner – Find an employee whose strengths offset another employee's weaknesses and team them together.
2. Training – Training will probably not turn weakness into strength, but it can get their performance up to more acceptable levels.

3. Shift roles – If the weakness is considered a fatal flaw, we may need to change the employee's responsibilities to shift focus away from their weaknesses. If we can't effectively do this within our company, an employee with a fatal flaw will may need to be let go.

"I feel like I've been lecturing a while so I should probably shut up and hear what you guys think," I interrupted myself.

The group seemed deep in thought. Rich finally broke the silence.

"It sounds logical; I'm just a bit concerned that we can really pull it off. I mean, if we only have people focused in areas of strength won't there be a bunch of stuff that won't get done. People can't spend 100 percent of their time only working at things they love to do and they're great at, can they?"

"I'm not suggesting we take this concept to the extreme," I answered. "We'll all need to continue to spend time in some areas that don't exactly play to our strengths. But, we should make a conscious effort to find ways to leverage people better than we are today. Today, we probably spend 80 percent of our time coaching our employees about their weaknesses and 20 percent of the time patting them on the back for the things they do well. I'm simply suggesting we reverse that equation. Most of our time should be spent coaching our team on how to leverage what makes them great. By doing that, we'll naturally start to get creative by partnering, training, and shifting roles."

LEVERAGE

"When you say 'leverage their strengths', do you just mean having them spend more time in those areas?" Joe asked.

"Great question Joe," I answered. "I think it means more than that. We could also leverage someone's strengths by having them help the rest of us improve in those areas. We may even want to leverage a strength by giving some additional tools or training in that area so they can go from being strong to being extraordinary."

"I think it's worth a try," Rich offered. "If we do this right, I've got to believe our folks would have a lot more passion for the job."

"We should rethink our recruiting and interviewing processes too," added Linda. "It sounds like we should focus a much greater portion of our screening and interviewing trying to find the right talents rather than focusing on a checklist of skills or experience."

"Great idea Linda. Now, to help us along, I've contracted with a personality assessment tool company. We all now have access to the tool, so let's start using it on ourselves and our teams. This ought to be a great help with the idea of *acceptance* we discussed last week, as well as *leverage.*

"In addition, I'd like each of you to meet with your individual team members again this week. The purpose of this meeting should be to discuss their strengths as well as the types of work they enjoy most. Then work with them to brainstorm some ways we can better leverage those areas. This may mean dramatically changing some job responsibilities."

PERFORMANCE BREAKTHROUGH

"We better be careful," Joe said sarcastically, "We've been meeting with our teams so much lately they may actually start to think we care about them."

The team still seemed a bit skeptical, but I really felt like we were on the right track.

* * *

LEVERAGE SUMMARY

Focus on, and leverage the strengths of, each individual on your team.

Focusing on weaknesses might help an employee become a bit more well-rounded, but, being well-rounded is incredibly overrated. Employees will rarely become strong in an area of weakness. The best you can hope for is that they will rise to become mediocre. However, where an employee has talent, they can become world-class. In addition, focusing on maximizing those areas where we have true talent is incredibly motivating.

This doesn't mean you should ignore weaknesses. By all means, if weaknesses are getting in the way of doing the job, you need to find ways to manage around those weaknesses. These can include looking for ways to get them to acceptable levels of performance, changing their responsibilities, or counseling them out of your organization. But don't expect them to become an expert tomorrow in those areas they're weak in today.

Your return on investment will be significantly greater by focusing your employee's efforts on continuing to build on their talents by adding new knowledge, experience, and tools. Would you rather have a well-rounded employee or a world-class employee?

"Starter" Ideas:

☑ **Hire for talent**
Modify hiring practices to ensure a well-rounded team, and not well-rounded individuals.

Most leaders create a list of skills and experiences they'd like a job candidate to have—things like: two years customer service experience, intermediate MS Word skills, apparel industry experience, etc.

Very few leaders have a feeling for what talents are required for the job. Talents are habits and tendencies that are wired into our brains from an early age—things like: leadership, flexibility, love of learning, or empathy.

Knowledge and skills can be learned and mastered through experience. Talents can rarely be taught and therefore should be hired in. If talents could be learned we'd all have the potential to be Michael Jordan.

The next time you're looking to fill a job opening, use the eighty-twenty rule. Spend 80 percent of your time defining and interviewing for talent and 20 percent on knowledge and skills.

☑ **Strengths-based performance planning**
Modify your annual performance evaluation process to:

- <u>Focus on strengths</u> instead of weaknesses. Use the process to identify strengths and passions, and determine how to better leverage those areas in the future.

- Initiate a <u>two-way discussion</u> versus a one-sided evaluation. Make it a forward-looking <u>planning</u> session instead of a backward-looking evaluation. Who cares what happened six months ago. The question is, what should we be doing differently in the future?

- Conduct <u>quarterly performance planning sessions.</u> Conducting these sessions quarterly will promote more of an ongoing dialogue, instead of a more formal annual or semi-annual evaluation.

☑ **Modify job descriptions**

Most companies create standard job descriptions and expect all of their employees to fit nicely inside that mold. While there are certainly some benefits to standard job descriptions, you'll find that some will tie your hands as you attempt to create a strengths-based team.

That doesn't mean creating unique job descriptions for each individual on your team. It simply means having an open mind to modify some responsibilities to better match people's strengths. It also means reviewing the strengths and weaknesses of your team before making hiring decisions. Recruit for talents your team is lacking, not necessarily for a well-rounded candidate.

☑ Spend more time with your best people

Most managers spend an inordinate amount of time with the poorest performers on the team. That might seem justified since those are the people that need our help the most. However, as counterintuitive as this seems, spending more time with your strongest performers actually provides the biggest opportunity for team growth.

Spending more time with your best people will help them grow from being strong at what they do to extraordinary. Working with your poorest performers will, in all likelihood, boost them from poor to mediocre. At the same time, by neglecting your strongest performers, over time, you're likely to see their performance start to dip. The end result is a mediocre team.

If you find yourself needing to spend a majority of time with poor performers, you may need to review your hiring practices and determine why these individuals are getting hired in the first place.

☑ Create flexible career paths

Sometimes the worst mistake you can make is promoting someone because they've done a great job in their current position.

The best example I've seen of this is promoting your best salesperson to sales manager. For many, the exact qualities that made them a great salesperson can make them a horrible sales manager. All at once, a company loses their best salesperson and hurts the productivity of the rest of the sales team.

What's wrong with growing forward instead of up? Allow your best sales people or your best customer service representatives to earn more while staying in those positions. To do this properly, you may need to create overlapping pay bands. In other words, create a pay range for more senior customer service representatives that allow them to make more than some junior supervisors.

* * *

ONE STEP FORWARD, TWO STEPS BACK

Four weeks had passed since John quit and I first met with the leadership team to discuss our issues. We hadn't solved our problems yet and our revenue was still anemic, but I was feeling more optimistic.

The leadership team seemed more passionate than I'd seen them since the early days and it seemed to be rubbing off on some of our employees. To keep the momentum, we needed a big win. A big win would give us all more confidence that the changes we were making were really making a difference.

No sooner than five seconds after that thought raced through my mind, the phone rang. I smiled at the phone before I picked it up, thinking "here it is…here's our big win…a new potential client calling? Vault Communications calling to say they changed their mind?" I picked up the phone and soon wished I hadn't.

Jim McClafferty, the CEO of Preston Blanc, one of our consumer products clients, was on the line. We had been working with them for about a year and they were our third largest client. We had just started the second phase of a financial systems implementation—a very large project that added some additional functions, reports, and bells and whistles to the software. We had no competition for winning that work since they were so happy with our work on the first phase. At that point, we had five consultants on the project, but it was planned to ramp up to between twelve and fifteen over the following few weeks.

"What can I do for you Jim?" I asked. Still confident this was going to be the good news we needed.

"Well Andy, your old friends from Vincore came to visit us last week and put a proposal on the table for our phase two financials project," Jim informed me without a hint of apology in his voice. "I've got to tell you, we were pretty impressed."

Almost unable to speak, I blurted, "Excuse me Jim; I'm not sure I heard you right. We've already started the project. You told me just last month you were so happy with phase one, you weren't asking anyone but us to propose on the project."

"That's true Andy. And I feel bad about it, but some things have changed over the last few weeks. Our board has put some pressure on us to implement a new inventory management system as well. Vincore heard about it and put a great offer on the table. They're willing to meet your price on the financials work as well as help us with our new inventory management system. They've got some great experience integrating those two systems. Last we spoke, I understood you guys hadn't implemented an inventory management system before. We need to work with a team that has experience in both."

I was in shock. Is that why John left to go to Vincore? To steal one of our best clients away?

"Jim, has the decision been finalized yet?"

"Not yet, but I intend to sign the contract within the next seven days."

"Do me a favor Jim, don't sign it before then. Give me a chance to put together a proposal that will blow you away. You trusted us with phase one of the financials project and you weren't disappointed. Trust us now and you won't regret it."

"All right, I guess I owe you that much. But Andy, I've got to be honest with you; I see a very small chance of you changing our minds."

"I understand. You'll have your new proposal before the week is up."

I hung up the phone, took a deep breath, crossed my arms on my desk, and buried my head in them.

It's amazing how your state of mind can change from optimism to pessimism in the span of a few minutes. Just when I was feeling we were starting to make some real progress, I realized that nothing had really changed. Not only were we still unprofitable, but we were about to lose another account.

Maybe I was putting too much stock into the "secrets" I'd learned from Dr. Moss. What business did I have trying to implement something meant for families into my business anyway? Businesses were much more sophisticated. What the heck was I thinking?

* * *

WORRY AND CONFUSION

It was already mid-afternoon so I decided to wait until the next day to tell the team about Preston Blanc. I wanted to get my act together and do some strategizing before I worked with them on a plan of attack.

Just then, Rich poked his head into my office.

"Andy, do you have a couple of minutes"

I took a deep breathe, trying to regain some control over my emotions. "Sure Rich, what's up?"

Rich came in and sat down. He looked down, deep thought for a moment, and then began. "I'm real worried Andy. I just found out my wife's expecting our first kid."

"That's great news Rich. Why are you worried? Is there a health issue or something?"

"No, that's not it. We plan on moving into a bigger place once the baby is born and, with the company going the way it is, I'm worried about my job."

I looked at Rich, not knowing what to say. I was worried too, so how could I lie to him and tell him everything would be okay. "I can't make any promises Rich. I know things don't look to good right now and things may get worse before they get better. We all just need to pull together and do our best."

"That's just it Andy. I really appreciate these leadership team meetings we've been having and I think our new ideas make sense. But I'm not sure I'm cut out for this stuff. I know I've been here two years but I still feel like the new guy. I've never been real good at getting to know people. Now I'm being asked to get to know my people better, their motivations, their strengths…I'm just not sure I can do it. My strength has always been technology, not people."

"I don't expect you to become something you're not Rich. If technology is your strength and your passion, we need to leverage that. Is there anyone on your team who has really strong people skills?"

Rich sat back and thought for a moment. "Sure, Sandy's great. She's pretty close with just about everyone on the team and seems to know what people are thinking before they do."

"Well, do you think you can work closer with Sandy and have her help you get know your people better? Maybe counsel with her when you need to make people related decisions?"

"I guess so. That's a real good idea. But, won't the rest of my team think it's unfair that I'm treating her special?"

"The more I think about the ideas of *acceptance* and *leverage*, the more I realize that our job is to treat everyone special. I know that sounds corny and I'm not even sure we can achieve it, but it needs to be our goal."

WORRY AND CONFUSION

Rich nodded, but still looked worried.

I was worried too…and confused. In the span of fifteen minutes I went from questioning if these "secrets" would help the business at all to using them to try to solve a business problem.

What we needed was a chance to put these ideas to the test. We also needed some good news to regain some momentum and give our people the confidence we'd survive.

* * *

QUADROPHENIA AGAIN

It was definitely time for some *Quadrophenia* during the ride home.

Right in the middle of "Love Reign O'er Me," my cell phone rang. It was my wife Susan calling to tell me Bobby's therapist cancelled that night's appointment and rescheduled for the following day. In the past, with other therapists, that would have been good news, but this guy was different. We'd made some good progress with Bobby over the last few weeks and, in addition, I was hoping he'd give me some magical insight into my latest business challenge. I guess I was on my own.

With my only plans for the evening cancelled, I decided to turn the car around and head back to the office for a late night of more strategizing as to how we'd save the Preston Blanc project. I had no solid ideas, but I had faith something would come to me after some good alone time. Alone time at the office meant I could do wacky things to get my idea juices flowing. I'd been known to run around the halls, sing, juggle, and even meditate.

After countless laps jogging around the office and throwing the stress ball against the wall for about thirty minutes, I decided to call my old friend John. I hadn't spoken to him since he left to go to Vincore. Maybe it was time to bury the hatchet.

"Guess who?" I said as if nothing had changed between us.

PERFORMANCE BREAKTHROUGH

"Andy, is that you? It's 9:30. Are you still in the office?

"Yeah…strange things like that happen when someone steals one of your major clients away," I said more playfully than serious.

"Andy, I'm so sorry about that. You need to know I had nothing to do with it. I wasn't even aware of it until yesterday. You know what a big machine this is; I'm not aware of half of what's going on around here."

"Don't worry about it John, I didn't call to blame you or get angry. How are things?"

"Things are good," John said unconvincingly. "Not much has changed from what you'd remember. They've got me going to Little Rock, Arkansas to speak to a few clients next week, and then to San Francisco the week after. I guess I'll be banking a lot of frequent flyer miles again."

"You don't sound overly enthusiastic."

"It's just been a long day, that's all. Believe me, things have been good. They've taken me back with open arms and given me a ton of responsibility. They've also implemented some great tools and methodologies since we left." He still wasn't very convincing, but I let it slide.

"How are things at A.M. Consulting?" he finally asked.

"Well, I'll be honest with you, losing you and Vault Communications in the same week was a big blow. We're still trying to recover, but I think we're starting to make some real progress."

"I've heard. I spoke with Kim the other day and she seemed pretty pumped about some changes you guys were making. She wouldn't tell me what they were but she said she loved your son's new therapist. What the hell was she talking about?"

"Trade secret John, but I'm glad to hear she's happy with our progress. You were right in some of the things you said before you left, about us losing our passion. We're just doing some things to rectify the situation."

John took a deep breath and there was a brief, awkward silence.

"Andy, I'm really sorry about the way things turned out. I feel like I let you down and…"

"John, stop," I interrupted. "You didn't do anything wrong. If I were you I probably would've done the same thing. More importantly, I just wanted to let you know we're about to win back the Preston Blanc account."

"How do you plan to do that?"

"Trade secret again, John. Let's keep in touch."

* * *

LIGHTENING BOLT

I got to the office at 7:15 a.m. as usual. I was feeling a bit better about things that morning. It struck me that, although the news from Preston Blanc was devastating, it might just be the lightening bolt we needed to inject some passion into the team again.

If we were to have a shot at winning back the account, we'd need to do two things. First, we'd need to come up with a creative sales strategy focusing on our competitive advantage; and second, we'd need to divide and conquer in a way that would maximize our effectiveness. This was a great time to make use of the ideas of *acceptance* and *leverage* we'd been discussing.

To finish our work on time we'd need to effectively motivate a pretty diverse team; that's where *acceptance* would come in. We needed to take what we'd learned from our teams over the last few weeks to come up with some creative ways to motivate and reward the folks participating on the proposal. We had some stressful work and long nights ahead of us and we'd need to ensure our team was pumped to do their best.

To most effectively divide and conquer, we'd need to assign people to those areas where they'd most likely hit the ball out of the park. We might need to change people's assigned reporting relationships and job descriptions to get the job done. I knew this might be difficult, but we needed to put our *leverage* idea to the test.

We'd need to use these ideas with the staff working on the proposal team as well as the leadership team. I began summarizing my thoughts on each of my direct reports; thoughts relating to how I needed to communicate to, and motivate each of them, as well as their individual strengths and how that would impact their roles on the proposal. The results were eye-opening and might ruffle some feathers initially, but I felt strongly my decisions would be best for the company.

I had made significant progress by about 9:30 a.m. so I decided to call an emergency leadership meeting to discuss the Preston Blanc situation and get started with the mountain of work we had ahead of us.

* * *

THE TEST

"I've got some good news and bad news," I began the meeting. "The good news is we've got an amazing chance to test the ideas we've been discussing over the last month. The bad news is, for the moment, Vincore has stolen away the Preston Blanc account."

You could almost hear the jaws dropping. No one spoke, so I decided to continue. I described my call with Preston Blanc's CFO and his explanation of why they decided to give the work to Vincore.

"So, basically we've got a week to win back the work. I've got a few ideas but I want to hear your thoughts. Any ideas?"

After another ten seconds of silence, Rich had a question. "Why did you say we've got a great chance to test the ideas we'd been discussing?"

"Well, we've got about a month's worth of work to do in seven days. I don't think we can attack this in a traditional way. We need to kick our team into a higher gear and we may need to adjust some of our normal responsibilities."

"I'm not sure what you mean, Andy," Kim interjected. "Preston Blanc is a consumer products client. That's my area of responsibility. Shouldn't it be up to me and my team to get this done?"

"Well...maybe, but let's think about it a minute," I answered. "When we discussed the idea of *leverage*, we agreed that focusing on everyone's strengths would allow us to optimize our performance. One way to do that would be to identify what talents we need to get the job done and then select and organize a team of individuals strongest in those areas, whether they're part of the consumer products team or not."

I knew this would be a difficult concept to grasp. We had never done business this way before. However, if we truly believed in the ideas we'd been discussing the past few weeks, we could turn concept into reality. I decided to pause to get Kim's reaction before continuing, since this impacted her the most.

Kim took a deep breath and seemed to take it all in. She looked off into the distance thoughtfully and seemed to come to a conclusion. She got up and walked over to the whiteboard.

"It seems to me we've got two key issues to deal with," she began writing. "First is the fact that Preston Blanc believes we have no inventory management expertise, and second, that we've never integrated their financials software package into an inventory management system. Do I have that right?"

"I would add a third," Linda offered. "Vincore is much bigger than we are and they're not going to let us win this project back without a fight. We're gonna need to completely blow Preston Blanc away just in case Vincore has anything else up their sleeve."

There were universal nods around the room.

THE TEST

Kim, still up at the whiteboard, continued; "Okay, let's deal with the issue of inventory management expertise first. I've got a few consultants who've done a little work in that area, but nothing real impressive. Anyone have any ideas?"

"I think we have an ace in the hole," I stood up and pointed at Linda. "There's no way Vincore can have anyone nearly as talented and experienced as Linda when it comes to analytics. Linda, didn't you do some inventory planning and control earlier in your career?"

"I can still execute an economic order quantity calculation in my sleep," she answered with a grin. "The computer systems may have changed, but I don't think the underlying logic has changed much in the last few years. If we bring on a contractor with the specific software knowledge, I can be the subject matter expert and chief number cruncher."

Joe looked confused, "But Linda's our controller; how can she work on a project?"

"We're leveraging strengths remember," Linda answered. "I'm sure Andy can find someone else to create our monthly financials while I'm saving the Preston Blanc account." It was great to have Linda on board with this, given her earlier attitude issues.

"Exactly right, Rich; do you have anyone on your tech team that could help with the integration issues?"

"Well, I don't think we have anyone that's worked with that specific package, but if we hire that contractor Linda mentioned, their specific software expertise and our data integration knowledge should give us the skills we need."

"Okay, here's the plan; Linda, you'll be inventory management subject matter expert and Rich, you'll head up the technical integration piece. Kim, you play the point and manage the entire proposal effort. Start looking into hiring the contractor we need as well. We'll need to put a name in the proposal. Let's also use what we learned about how our individual team members are motivated to come up with some enticing rewards if we sell this one. We'll need to put in some long days and nights over the next week to pull this off and we'll need everyone at their best."

Joe was looking a bit dejected since he was not part of the action plan. That wouldn't last long.

"Joe, it looks like it's up to you and me to start on the next part of our master plan," I said, grinning and rubbing my hands together like an evil genius.

* * *

THE THIRD SECRET

The following day it was time for our third session with Dr. Moss. I never thought I'd see the day when I'd be anxious for a therapy session, but given the family and business results I'd seen thus far, it was a very different situation.

Things at home were better than they had been in a long time. I'm not sure I'd call it consistent progress—kids with Asperger's defy the word consistent—but there was certainly a lot less yelling around the house.

Our business problems were still massive, but I was definitely starting to see more passion from my leadership team, as well as the staff. We still had a long way to go, but I was more optimistic than I'd been in a while.

Again, the session started with a discussion of the wins we had seen thus far. Then, Dr. Moss introduced the third secret; he called this one *impact*.

Impact focused on ensuring Bobby had a level of control or ownership over his life. He needed to feel like we trusted him enough to allow him to have a significant impact on the decisions that affected him. This secret built on the first two; if we accepted Bobby for what made him unique (*acceptance*) and focused on his strengths (*leverage*), we should be able to trust him enough to make the right choices (*impact*). Trust was the key word.

PERFORMANCE BREAKTHROUGH

The truth was, given Bobby's low maturity level and our low boiling point, we didn't give him an inch. We spent a significant part of our lives, and his, waiting for him to do something wrong. Dr. Moss helped us realize that we were basically on top of him every waking moment, and entrusting him with very little.

We discussed some ways to gradually introduce this concept into our lives. We would start with small decisions like, "Do you want to eat dinner at 6:00 or 6:30?" or "What type of hair style do you want?" Then we would slowly graduate to more important things like when to work on school projects, what summer camp to go to, or which chores he wanted to do around the house.

I've got to be honest, this secret scared me more than the first two. I wasn't sure Bobby was up to making mature decisions. If we weren't careful, he'd wind up playing Nintendo and eating cheese doodles from sun up to sun down. Well, I'd trusted the therapist thus far and he hadn't steered us wrong so I thought I'd throw caution to the wind and give it a shot.

It goes without saying that Bobby loved this idea more than we did. As the therapist described the concept, Bobby had this grin on his face and kept looking at me as if to say, "Who's the boss now?"

We were either making progress or in big trouble.

* * *

BATTLES

We were two days into our seven day Preston Blanc proposal marathon and things were not going smoothly. Not that I expected it was going to be easy. To top that off, most of us knew that losing that account could spell the beginning of the end for our company.

In my opinion, we were chugging along at about sixty percent productivity. I calculated that using a simple formula of subtracting the forty percent of the time my team was fighting each other from a possible productivity of one hundred percent. I was trying very hard not to get discouraged; we had built up some great momentum over the past few weeks and I didn't want to lose it at exactly the wrong time. Don't get me wrong, everyone was trying to do the right thing, but tensions get high when people are sleep deprived and work overloaded.

The latest battle was between Kim and Rich. I was taking my five minute lunch break at my desk when Rich poked his head in. "Andy you busy?" he asked as he walked in and took a seat, not really waiting for my answer.

"Always time for you Rich, what's up?"

"I need your help dealing with Kim. I know you put her in charge of the proposal effort and, don't get me wrong, I agree that she's the right one for the job, but she's driving me nuts!" As he said this he got up and started pacing across the room. Rich was trying hard not to lose control, but I could tell he was really stressed about it.

"Rich, tell me specifically what happened?"

"My team and I are trying to come up with estimates for the financial interface...which is a ton of work. At the same time, I'm trying to find a contractor with the software skills we need. I've done this before, and so has my team, but Kim feels like she needs to be involved in everything. I can't make a move without her injecting some new thought or idea. She's also causing a bottleneck because she wants to be involved in every meeting. It's slowing us down and driving me crazy!"

I can't say this came as a shock. I put Kim in charge of the proposal because she gave us the best chance of winning the work. She was incredibly bright and knew how to get the job done, no matter what. However, I also knew that some strengths, taken to an extreme, could be a weakness. Kim could sometimes leave bodies in her wake.

This wasn't just an issue with Kim, however. That morning, I saw Linda and her staff going at it in the hallway about her keeping them on too short a leash. The rest of us had similar issues with each other and our staffs. Funny how we all felt overworked, but we still felt the need to not only do our own work, but look over everyone else's shoulder.

This had been a running theme at A.M. Consulting for a long time, and not just the past two days. The level of distrust and micromanagement was an obstacle we needed to do something about immediately.

And, as usual, my son's therapist gave me the answer.

"I understand Rich. I'll get it resolved quickly. Leave it to me."

* * *

JOE

Before I dealt with Rich's issue, I needed to take Joe to lunch and do some additional team planning.

"Okay Andy, when are you gonna tell me about phase two of this master plan of yours?" he said as the hostess seated us.

"Remember we talked about leveraging strengths the other day?"

Joe nodded

"What do you think your biggest strength is?"

"Well," Joe sat back and thought a bit, "no one in our firm knows telecommunications technology better than me. And my knowledge of the utilities industry is real strong. You know, I've given some keynotes at a few industry conferences and the participants were always impressed with my insights."

"All true," I answered, "but what do you think your one greatest strength is? Why do you think you're such an asset to our company?"

Joe sat back in his chair a bit and looked up at the ceiling for some inspiration. "I guess I'm not sure Andy; what do you think?"

I could have told him what I thought, but I thought it'd be more powerful if I let him figure it out. "Those keynotes you mentioned…how did you get those?"

"Oh, that was easy. I got the one last May because I knew a few of the folks on the organizing committee. I met them at a conference a few years ago. We developed a pretty good relationship and I stayed in touch.

"I got the one in November because I knew the CEO at one of the conference's gold level sponsors. He and I have played golf together at a few networking events."

"Still don't know what your biggest strength is?" I asked.

He looked confused. "I guess I'm still not sure what you're getting at."

"You said getting those keynotes was easy, but it's not. Sometimes we're blind to our greatest strength because we think everyone can do it. Think again about how you got those keynotes."

Joe sat back and took a breath. After about a minute of staring into space, he seemed to finally get it. "Oh, do you mean my network?"

"Bingo," I answered. "You're always the one I count on to know someone. Need an early tee time, you know someone. Need a ticket to the game, you know someone. Need a plumber, you know someone."

JOE

"I guess I always just took that for granted. Ever since I was a kid I was the type that had a lot of friends and always kept in touch with people, even if I hadn't seen them in years. I never thought of that as a strength, It was just something I liked to do."

"The real question is, how do we take advantage of that strength? Over the last few weeks, we've lost the Vault Communications account and Preston Blanc is hanging on by a string. The question is, who do you know?"

* * *

IMPACT

Although the leadership team was hard at work on the Preston Blanc proposal, I thought the latest lesson from Dr. Moss warranted a little break in the action.

We had a ton of work to do and wouldn't have time for the typical hand-holding and micromanagement. Maybe it was time we truly trusted people to do their jobs. Maybe a discussion about the third secret would come at exactly the right time.

"Andy, I know you've been on this leadership meeting kick, but we've got our hands full. Can we make this one quick?" Kim groaned as she walked in the room.

Rich joined in, "I second that. I've got a day filled with contractor interviews before I can even start my real work. I told my wife not to expect to see me for a while."

"I get it guys. We're all working our butts off, but this is important. I saw my son's therapist again last night."

"Uh oh, this is gonna take a while," Linda said sarcastically, but with a smile.

"I promise this new idea will save us all some time," I said trying to gain back some control. "Sit down, relax, and hear me out."

"This next secret is called *impact*." I continued, "And before I describe it, I'd like to ask you all a question. Is there one right way to do a job?"

"Of course not," Joe answered.

"Why not?"

"Because we're all different," he continued. "The ideas of *acceptance* and *leverage* stressed that. If we all have different motivations, learning styles, strengths, and passions, it would seem to me that the most effective method for me to get a job done may not work as well for you, Linda, Kim, or Rich."

I couldn't have said it better myself. "Okay, thanks Joe. So our way may not always be the best way, but let's take this idea a step further. When you're meeting with your teams, how often do you tell instead of ask?"

Seeing confused looks, I clarified. "If you're sitting around a table with your team and you've got a problem to solve, do you normally dictate the answer or ask the team to help you figure things out?"

"Well, I ask sometimes but they don't have the broad perspective I have on a lot of these issues," Linda answered defensively. "Most of the time it's quicker for me to just tell them what I need them to do. I mean, I explain it to them, but I'm their boss. They should trust me to have the right answer."

IMPACT

"I agree with Linda," Kim offered. "As a leadership team, we're supposed to have the answers, right? I mean, that's why we're here. That's why you put us in these positions."

"Actually, you're all in leadership positions because you're the people I trust to get the job done. I don't necessarily expect you to have all the answers all the time. I just know, somehow, you'll find a way.

"Okay, so you've got a challenge or a problem and you sit your team down and you say 'Okay guys, we've got this problem, so here's what we're gonna do; Bill, you do X, Jane, you do Y, and Steve, you do Z.' Is that right?"

"In so many words, yeah," Kim replied.

"So now Bill goes and does what you told him to do, but he hits an obstacle; what does he do now?"

Kim was a bit confused; "I'm not sure what you mean."

"Well, if your idea didn't work, what will Bill do next? Will he jump over the obstacle, run around it, or knock it down?"

"None of those; they usually come back to me with an attitude of 'Okay genius, what do I do now?'"

"That's exactly my point, Kim." I stood for emphasis. "When we dictate the answers to our teams, they lose the ability to think on their own. In that same situation, what would happen if you asked your team what they thought? I mean, even if you were ninety nine percent sure you knew the right answer, what if you asked your team anyway and encouraged a productive conversation?"

Linda was getting a bit frustrated. "But if you already know the answer why would you waste time asking your team and having a long conversation?"

Joe decided to enter the fray. "That's short-term thinking, Linda. If we discuss it with our teams, it becomes the whole team's solution, not just ours. Don't we want our teams owning the decision, rather than just carrying out our orders?"

"Right Joe," I interrupted. "If the team owns the decision, they'll do whatever it takes to jump over, run around, or smash through any obstacle in their way. They'll feel like they have some latitude to make decisions so they don't always have to come back to one of us for further instructions. They'll also start to learn to think on their own and take some initiative."

"Also, as much as I hate to admit it," Rich added, "I'm not always the smartest guy in the room. There are times my team may have a better answer than me. I'll never know it if I don't ask them."

"So by asking instead of telling we win either way," I summed up. "Whether our idea was best or not, we win because everyone buys in and we get the best answer. Being the boss doesn't mean you're always the smartest person in the room. Being the boss doesn't mean you need to make all the decisions.

And being the boss doesn't mean you have all the answers."

"So does that mean we need to make sure everyone on our team agrees before we move forward with a decision?" Linda asked skeptically.

"No, it just means we need to stop letting our ego get the best of us. It means we stop dictating decisions to our team and ask them for advice. This doesn't mean management by consensus. Ultimately, as a leader, you need to make the final decision, but it's critical to make your team part of the process. Even if you think you know the answer, ask your team what they think first, before dictating a decision."

I then drew the following chart on the whiteboard.

Dictatorial Management	Participatory Management
Your team's effectiveness is limited by your vision and knowledge.	Allows the team to rise higher as all team members' talents are used to the team's advantage.
Your team will become paralyzed if you're not available to make a decision.	Allows the team to make effective decisions with or without you.
You feel ownership for all decisions.	Allows the team to make effective decisions with or without you..

"Okay, I buy it," said Kim, "but when we started this discussion, you said it would save us all some time. It seems to me that having these discussions might take more time, not less."

"Well, let's think about that a bit," I said, hoping to tie all of this together by relating it to the battles we had over the past few days. "In order to have a more participatory company and allow our people to feel like they have true ownership and impact on the bottom line, how does our attitude toward our people need to change?"

There were some confused looks around the table. After a long silence, Joe finally offered, "I'm not sure if this is what you're getting at, but we need to treat our people with more respect. They're not just robots following instructions."

"Excellent; what else?"

"I think we need to trust them more," Rich answered.

"Say more about that Rich," I prodded.

"Well, if we're going to allow them to have a greater role in the decision making process, we need to trust them." Rich seemed to be on a role now. "We need to stop defining every step they need to take to get something done. Maybe our role should be focused more on defining outcomes and give them more responsibility for figuring out the best way to get there. They're working on the front lines everyday so they're probably smarter than we are when it comes to the real detail anyway."

"So, to answer Kim's question, how does all this relate to us saving time?

"Let me ask you this, Kim," I challenged, "how much time have we all wasted this week because of our distrust of one other?"

"What's that supposed to mean? I trust you guys!" Kim took offense.

I realized my question came off a bit harsh, but I really wanted to make a point. I was about to answer Kim when Rich jumped in.

IMPACT

"How can you say that, Kim? You've been all over me and my team the last couple of days. If you trusted us, you'd let us do our jobs and you wouldn't feel the need to be part of every decision."

"That has nothing to do with lack of trust, Rich." Kim was visibly flustered. "It's just that as the leader of this proposal effort it's my job to make sure we're doing the best job we possibly can. How can I do that if I'm not involved?"

"I have no problem with you being involved," Rich answered, "but your need to be a part of every decision is really causing us a bottleneck. I think that's what Andy means when he says the idea of *impact* will save us time. We've got three weeks worth of work to do in the next five days. We don't have the time to make sure everyone is at every meeting and everyone signs off on every little thing."

"I didn't realize you guys felt that way. I really didn't mean for anyone to think I didn't trust them," Kim said apologetically.

With the point made, I decided to jump back in. "It's not just you, Kim. It's all of us. I've been doing the same thing for years, not just the last couple of days. It's hard to let go, but we need to allow each other, and our teams, to reach our potential. We never will unless we trust them enough to do their jobs the way that works best for them."

"But what if we know our team is doing the wrong thing? Do we just shut up and watch them fail?" Linda challenged.

"Absolutely not," I answered. "This doesn't mean we shouldn't provide some guidance up front or assistance down the road if things get off track. It just means we give people a lot more rope than we have been.

"It also means we encourage our people to challenge us, their teammates, and the process. That's going to mean more conflict, but it'll be productive conflict. I believe better ideas will come out of this conflict. People will only feel comfortable engaging in conflict, however, if we trust them and they trust us."

"You know, it's interesting how each of these ideas seem to be building on the one before," Joe offered.

"What do you mean?" I asked.

"Well, the first secret, *acceptance,* taught us that we needed to get to know our people at a much deeper level; learn what makes them tick. By doing that, we were able to understand and maximize their strengths using the second secret, *leverage.* And now that we've got people more focused on what they do best, we should be able to trust they'll do their jobs at a very high level. That allows us to achieve the third secret by giving them the ability to have more *impact* on our decisions and bottom line everyday."

I was impressed. "Very well said, Joe. Hey, why are you guys all sitting around? We've got a client to win back. Let get back to work!"

* * *

IMPACT SUMMARY

Define outcomes, not steps. Be participatory, not dictatorial.

Conventional management wisdom advises that you'll get the most out of your employees by defining specific goals and detailed procedures for getting there. This is only half right. Creating challenging goals is critical. However, you should let your employees figure out how to get there.

Most of us know it's the people on the front lines who truly understand the best way to get things done. Defining every detailed procedure for them not only stifles their motivation and creativity, but also lowers the chance they'll create break-through performance.

If you've hired the right people and given them the tools necessary to do the job, you should give them the freedom to get the job done. Giving them ownership will allow them to reach their true potential.

"Starter" Ideas:

☑ **Conduct team-driven goal setting**
Good leaders and managers set goals for their team and create an accountability structure to manage and measure results. Exceptional leaders take that idea one step further by allowing the team to set their own

goals, which will them feel more ownership and more accountability towards their accomplishment.

A team-driven goal setting process can work as follows:

- ☑ Conduct a team planning meeting where you focus on two objectives:
  - Ensure the team understands the organizational vision and strategic goals or initiatives. If your organization does not have a vision and a set of strategic goals or initiatives, create them before moving forward.
  - Ask your team to work together over the next week to identify four to eight key metrics that will drive the team towards the accomplishment of the organizational goals (i.e. number of sales meetings, number of new clients, number of referrals, customer retention rate, etc.). For each metric, they should also work together to set team and/or individual goals.
- ☑ Conduct a follow-up team planning meeting to review the metrics and goals your team has come up with. Push back if you're uncomfortable with either the metrics or the specific goals. Make sure your team is aggressive, but not unrealistic. Just because your team is setting their own goals doesn't mean you shouldn't provide strong guidance when necessary.

IMPACT SUMMARY.

☑ **Conduct more participatory team meetings**
Part of planning for any team meeting should be identifying a few key questions to ask your team. It might
take the form of advice on new product or service, res-
olution of key issue, or setting of a team goal.

Most leaders spend much more time identifying what
they'd like to dictate in the meeting and very little time
determining the best ways to encourage discussion
and participation.

☑ **Encourage more ideas from your team**
Do this by:

- Asking for suggestions (i.e. What are the five
  dumbest things we do? What should we do
  more of? What should we stop doing?).
- Focusing on ways to reward intelligent failure
  rather than punish for mistakes made.
- Conducting open forum meetings to discuss
  events, ideas and issues.
- Following up on suggestions consistently.

☑ **Be vulnerable**
It's okay for managers to say "I made a mistake" or "I'm
not very good at that." Being vulnerable with your
team will dramatically increase their level of trust in
you. They will also feel more comfortable sharing their
vulnerabilities with you. Productive communications
amongst your team will skyrocket.

☑ **Encourage arguments**

Does your team get along great?

Do you always seem to agree with each other?

Do you have trouble remembering your last major team conflict?

This may seem strange, but if you answered yes to these questions, you've got problems. A team needs conflict to evolve.

Think of it as Darwin's theory of evolution for business. If good ideas don't crush bad ideas, and great ideas don't crush good ideas, a business, and its employees, will grow stagnant and die.

* * *

A STEP FORWARD

The hard work had really paid off. Our Preston Blanc proposal blew away any client presentation we had ever conducted before. We had all the angles covered and created incredible rapport with the client, especially, their CEO, Jim McClafferty. The client team actually applauded when we were done…I've never seen that happen after presenting a proposal before.

We also had an ace in the hole. It turned out that Joe knew someone who knew someone on the board of Preston Blanc. Through that contact, we were able to find out about a Preston Blanc hot button we never knew about before. It seemed that they were trying to win a big account of their own and Joe (God love him) knew the CEO of that company. Their sons went to summer camp together. To make a long story short, Joe was able to work some magic and take both CEOs out to dinner. The conversation was great and really helped Preston Blanc make major strides in winning the account. Playing matchmaker helped us to solidify a more strategic relationship with Jim McClafferty. It also didin't hurt to have the law of reciprocity working on our side. I guess that discussion with Joe about leveraging his strengths really paid off.

More importantly, though, that process really helped us come together as a team. Using the ideas of acceptance, leverage, and impact, we now understood each other better, maximized our strengths, and trusted each other more than ever before. I was really feeling good about things, and so was my leadership team. Our positive attitudes seemed to be having an effect on the rest of the office as well. The air in the office seemed to be lighter somehow.

Three days after the proposal I was expecting a call from Jim McClafferty. He promised to call to let us know their decision. Would we win our big client back or would we lose the big fish to Vincore?

* * *

Thirty minutes later, I had my leadership team assembled in the conference room. No one said a word. They just looked at me, knowing I called them together because I had some news.

"I just got a call from Jim McClafferty. We had a nice talk and he really appreciated our efforts on the proposal." I looked around at my team, showed no hint of emotion, and paused for dramatic effect. "I wanted to thank you and your teams as well; you all did a great job. I really felt we came together as a team like I haven't seen for a long time." I paused again and looked around at the team.

Linda had just about enough of this and said, "Andy, cut the garbage. Did we win the work or not?"

"Oh, I almost forgot," I smiled. "We start next Tuesday."

All at once, the team jumped up and started screaming, hugging, and high-fiving each other. I hadn't seen that kind of passion from this team in a while. Come to think of it, I don't think I had ever seen that kind of passion; even in the early days.

"I don't want to keep you guys long," I said as things calmed down a bit. "I'd like to let you go tell your teams about this fantastic win. And let's try to take off early today, we all deserve it. Before I let you go, I really want to thank each of you for the work you all did to make this happen. I want to make sure you all realize what an incredible team effort this really was.

"Kim, without you spearheading the proposal effort and managing all of us to meet some incredible deadlines, we never would have made this sale.

"Linda, the lack of inventory management skills was the reason we almost lost this account. Your analytical skills really saved the day.

"Rich, the technical integration of the inventory management component was just as important, and you pulled off an incredibly effective design in record time.

"And Joe, getting us a great contact on the Preston Blanc board and then using it to add value so quickly was really like pulling a rabbit out of a hat.

"I'm really proud of all of you. Now go spread the good word and go home and get some rest!"

* * *

BACK IN BLACK

Selling, or should I say reselling, the Preston Blanc account was like taking a thousand-pound weight off of my shoulders. Don't get me wrong, we still had a long way to go, but for the first time in a while, I felt like things were trending up. Instead of seeing employees leave or having to let them go, we were actually back in hiring mode.

From back in my Vincore days, it became a tradition for me to take the family out to P.F. Chang's for dinner whenever I sold some new work. That night was definitely a P.F. Chang's night.

If you check the *Guinness Book of World Records*, you'll find that our car ride to the restaurant that night was the loudest car ride on record. Although my singing voice is nothing special, I loved to sing along to my favorite music in the car, and once I started, my family liked to join in. Tonight it was AC/DC's *Back in Black*. By the time we got to P.F. Chang's our throats were sore, but we were all in a great mood.

When we were seated for dinner, I looked around at my family. For a moment, it was as if I was watching a video of some family I used to know. They were talking and laughing and having a genuinely great time with one another. It felt fantastic.

The last couple of years had been difficult. The stresses of difficult times financially and trying to manage Bobby's Apserger's had really taken a toll on the family. Susan and I were near our boiling point all the time; quick to anger, at the kids and at each other. We spent too much time saying no to things we wanted to do because of money issues. We spent too much time yelling at Bobby instead of helping him. I was worried about what that was doing to him as well as the impact it was having on Jenny.

All of that meant we were spending less quality time together as a family. Even when we were together and not fighting, too often it was different family members doing different things in different rooms. Together, yet very apart.

That night I felt a change. Like we had turned a corner and were becoming a family again. Things were nowhere near perfect, and never would be. Bobby's Asperger's syndrome wasn't, and never would be cured. He would always have difficulties with his social skills and impulse control. He would never grow up to match the dreams I had for him when he was a baby. But that was okay. We'd learned to accept him for who he was, strategize ways for him to leverage his strengths, and trust that he was doing his best.

I also still had a long way to go at work to strengthen the company and get us on more solid ground. We had won back a big account, but we were still smaller than we were the previous year. We needed to start growing again and I needed to start earning a comfortable living again.

Becoming the perfect company or the perfect family wasn't the point. The point was that we were all striving to improve our family and our company every day. And, for the first time in a long time, we were doing it with incredible optimism for the future.

THE FOURTH SECRET

Two nights later, it was time for our next appointment with Dr. Moss.

As usual, we started by talking about some wins we'd had since our last session. We discussed some good things that were going on at home, including our decision to leverage the kids strengths by enrolling Bobby in video game design camp and Jenny in dance camp. Getting the kids to talk in these sessions was usually like pulling teeth; however, they were more than willing to talk endlessly about their respective camps.

We also discussed how we'd used the third secret of *impact,* with the kids by letting them plan some monthly outings for the family and decide what we were having for dinner once a week.

I even mentioned some things going on at work. I thanked him for his counsel, but told him I wasn't going to pay him double for helping me professionally, as well as personally.

We then discussed the fourth secret. It was called *celebration* and it was timed perfectly after our P.F. Chang's dinner.

Dr. Moss explained that to continue the momentum we had gained, we needed to create a constant flow of positive energy as a family by having fun and celebrating our accomplishments, big and small. We would not be able to sustain the progress we'd made using the first three secrets unless we were all motivated to keep moving forward.

First, we discussed focusing more time on what the kids did right and praising them for it. Not just the big things (great report cards from school, awards, etc.), but the small things as well.

The praise had to be both timely and specific in order to be meaningful. A great way to implement this idea was to create games to reward the kids for good behavior. One specific idea we came up with for Bobby was to give him more video game time if he did extra reading or exercise. The most powerful way to implement this idea, however, was to give the kids informal feedback (a pat on the back, saying good job) when they did little things, which for Bobby might include getting up on time in the morning without being told, or trying a new food.

We next discussed finding more ways to play as a family. This would not only create more of a positive atmosphere at home but would encourage us to spend a lot more time together as well. We decided to go on at least one full-day family outing every month. We also decided to have a family game night once a week.

The kids were obviously ecstatic about this new secret. Susan and I were pretty excited as well. Too often, life felt like a constant struggle to get through the day. The first three secrets had helped us make a ton of progress, but what's the point if we were not enjoying life along the way.

* * *

CELEBRATION

One week had gone by since winning the Preston Blanc account and it was time for our next leadership team meeting. The excitement had died down a bit since the big win and the reality of the hard work ahead of us set in. The atmosphere was still positive, but if we weren't careful, the feelings would be short-lived.

"So," I started the meeting. "Are we having fun yet?"

"Did someone spike your coffee this morning, Andy?" Linda joked.

"I'm not that lucky, Linda." I tried again; "I mean it. Are we having fun?"

"We're at work, Andy, it's not supposed to be fun," Linda pushed back, a bit more seriously this time. "We're supposed to get the job done and then leave. It's after we leave that the fun usually starts."

"This is a strange start to our meeting this morning," Kim added. "Something tells me you saw the great Dr. Moss again."

"As a matter of fact, I did. And he shared the fourth and final secret with us last night. It's called *celebration*."

Usually, when the team heard I was about to share one of Dr. Moss's secrets, there were groans, since they knew it would be a longer meeting. This time, they all sat forward a bit in anticipation. They actually seemed excited.

"Okay, hit us with it," said Rich.

"When I asked if you guys were having fun, you thought I was joking, but I wasn't." I continued; "We spend half our waking lives at work. Shouldn't we figure out how to make it fun?"

"Dr. Moss's other secrets were great Andy, but I don't think this one really fits," Joe argued. "We're too busy to worry about having fun. We're just trying to get through the day, meet our deadlines, and still find a way to see our families and get some sleep."

"I agree," Kim added. "Maybe we should wait until we're not so busy to discuss this one."

"I, for one, hope that day never comes," I argued. "I don't ever want us to NOT be busy at work again. It's no fun when business is slow; we're all too busy worrying about the company and our jobs. The time to celebrate and have fun is now, when things are going well."

"Pardon me for asking a stupid question," Linda interjected. "Why is it so important we have fun? We're here to get a job done, not to have a great time. Andy, you don't pay us to play, you pay us to work."

CELEBRATION

Rich jumped in to save me. "Hold on guys. I understand what Andy's trying to say. Let's not dismiss this so quickly. If our work environment was more fun, our employees would be happier right?"

Everyone nodded at the obvious question.

"Well, if our employees are happier, wouldn't that make them more creative and more willing to work hard? Wouldn't their positive attitudes impact the level of service they provided our clients?"

"It also wouldn't hurt our recruiting efforts," Joe interjected. "If our people are having more fun at work, they'd be like talent magnets. They'd refer more people to work here and as other people heard about our company, they'd seek us out as well."

"That all sounds great, but how do we do that when we're so busy?" Linda asked, bringing us down to earth.

"We plan for it, that's how," I answered forcefully and stood up for emphasis. "We make it a priority. We always seem to find the time for an important client meeting or the completion of some deliverable. Why can't we find the time to plan a fun event or praise someone for a job well done? If we don't find ways to inject more positive energy into the office, I'm afraid people will burn out, and that includes us."

"Okay, you convinced me," conceded Kim. "The concept makes sense, but how do we apply it? What specifically did you have in mind?"

Linda surprised everyone with an idea. "We could give out an award for anyone that goes above and beyond their job description to help a client or coworker. My daughter does something like this at her company. I think they call it the ABCD Award, which stands for 'Above and Beyond the Call of Duty.'"

It was a great idea and everyone was shocked it came out of Linda's mouth. She was definitely not someone we looked at to spearhead anything fun. We looked at her in amazement.

"Don't be so shocked," she said. "I have a fun side. I've just never shown it to you guys."

When the laughter died down, I added, "I think that's a great idea Linda, and I want to add a thought. I don't think the award should come from us. I think we should set it up so anyone could nominate anyone for the award: boss to subordinate, peer to peer, or subordinate to boss. We could create an ABCD committee whose job it is to review all of the nominations and select the best one every month. This way it won't seem like the typical employee of the month, top-down, kiss-butt type of award."

Kim had and idea as well. "What about doing a community service day for the entire office. I'm sure we'd be able to find a charity that could use our help for the day doing something like cleaning up a neighborhood or teaching underprivileged kids about business. We'd be doing something good for the community, having fun, and doing some team building at the same time."

Now it was Joe's turn. "We should get together with our teams more after work too. Sometimes just hanging out with people socially helps create stronger relationships."

CELEBRATION

"Linda looked concerned. "I'm not so sure that's a good idea. I like to keep a professional relationship with my team. Once it gets personal, things can get difficult. What if I need to fire one of my folks? It makes it much harder if I feel like I'm friends with them."

"I don't think we need to be friends with our staff" Joe countered. "We just need to create a relationship where we can be more open and honest with each other…dealing with people on a more personal level. Breaking down that professional brick wall we have with a lot of our folks may do us and them some good."

The conversation had really gained some momentum and it was my turn to add an idea. "These are great ideas guys and I think we need to do some more informal things as well. Sometimes the most important thing we can do is to remember to pat someone on the back or thank them for a job well done. It's easy to do, but how many of us do it consistently? What if we made a conscious decision to do it more often? We could even get a bunch of thank you cards and give them to people when they do a good job, just to let them know how much we appreciate them."

We spent another forty five minutes debating some really strong ideas. By the end of the meeting we had six solid ideas and key action items for their implementation.

Skeptical at first, the team was now really energized by the discussion. This was just what we needed to keep up our momentum. Thank you again, Dr. Moss.

CELEBRATION SUMMARY

There's a reason why teams play better in front of a home-town crowd. There's a reason why stand-up comics feed off the laughter of the crowd. Appreciation works!

Find ways to measure and reward positive outcomes. Compliment and celebrate your team's accomplishments big and small. Reward activity, not just financial performance. There's no such thing as too much praise, as long as it's genuine.

Find ways to have fun as a team. Fun breed creativity, collaboration, trust and productivity.

"Starter" Ideas:

☑ **Ways to reward and/or praise your team:**
  - <u>Above and Beyond the Call of Duty (ABCD) Award</u> – Reward people for doing something outside of the scope of their job to help a client, coworker, or supplier. Nominations for this award can be made by anyone (supervisor, co-worker, or subordinate).
  - <u>Employee dollars</u> – Give out fake money when an employee is caught doing something great. This money can only be redeemed for work related privileges or gifts (time off, gift to their favorite charity, etc.).

- <u>Visibility</u> – Praise people in a way that gives them more visibility within the organization. You can mention them in the company newsletter, give them an appreciation lunch, or recognize them at a company event.

- <u>Include the family</u> – Reward an employee by taking that person, and their families, out to lunch, dinner, or a show. Including the family adds a nice, personal touch which will be greatly appreciated.

- <u>Education/personal growth</u> – Offer to send people to a seminar, workshop, or hire a coach for them. This will show appreciation and improve their productivity at the same time.

- <u>Thank you notes</u> – Show your appreciation by sending a thank you note immediately following a job well done.

☑ **Ways to have fun with your team:**

  ☑ <u>Themed work environment</u> – Create fun, themed work environments periodically. These themes can include things like:

- *Music* – Play upbeat music in the office.
- *Games* – Have games around like Scrabble, Pictionary, Trivial Pursuit, etc.
- *Masquerade party* – Dress up as your favorite coworker.
- *Sports* – Wear something from your favorite sports team.

  ☑ <u>Social events/parties</u> – Getting together socially, as a team, for dinner, drinks, a sporting event, etc.

can have an enormous bonding effect on a team. Getting to know people personally can improve trust and make for much more effective working relationships.

☑ Community service day – Plan a day for the entire company, or a team, to perform a community service activity.

☑ Make noise – Give everyone on the team a unique noisemaker (kazoo, bell, harmonica, etc.). Tell them to use the noisemaker whenever something good happened. Make a sale, use the noisemaker. Meet a goal, use the noisemaker.

☑ Make "fun" a value and/or a mission – Many organizations have a defined set of values (i.e. integrity, collaboration, respect, etc.) and a mission statement. Including fun in values and/or the mission statement will ensure it stays a high priority.

* * *

CONTINUED PROGRESS

The next three months at A.M. Consulting were the most productive since the birth of the company three years prior. We picked up two new clients, hired five new consultants, and our pipeline of new prospective clients was bigger than ever. Most importantly, I was actually looking forward to going to work again.

We were still holding our weekly leadership team meetings. That morning, I had two announcements to make that would continue our momentum and, possibly, kick us into the next gear.

"So, are we having fun?" I started every leadership team meeting that way now. It was my way of asking the team what good stuff had happened since we last met.

The team proceeded to give me some updates regarding two new prospective clients, one new project starting up the following week, and some new recruiting activities that were underway.

"How's our new leadership development program going?" I asked Linda.

"We should be ready, as scheduled, to have our managers start the program next week," she answered.

PERFORMANCE BREAKTHROUGH

This was a new program we decided to implement based on the four secrets we learned and implemented so successfully. Our goal was to help our managers develop the necessary habits to implement the ideas with their staff. I told Dr. Moss about the program and he actually offered to address the group during the kickoff meeting.

"I have two announcements to make that I think you'll all be real excited about." Only one other person in the room knew what I was about to say.

"First, we're back in the running to win some very significant work at Vault Communications.

"We need to thank Joe for all of his hard work and really making it happen," I continued. "Joe, tell them how you did it?"

"Well, it turns out my son's little league baseball coach has a brother on the Vault executive team. I was able to get a meeting with him and it went well. What really clinched it though was when I gave him a tour of our offices last week. He couldn't believe how much all of our people really seemed to care about our clients. He said he saw incredible passion here. I couldn't believe he said that, since the lack of passion was exactly why we lost the work last time."

The team applauded Joe for a job well done.

"While the focus is on Joe, I have another announcement to make that concerns him," I said as I walked over and gave him a pat on the back.

CONTINUED PROGRESS

"As you all know, since John left, I've been acting as our director of business development. That will end today. Since Joe has done an incredible job helping us win back the Preston Blanc account and now, hopefully, Vault Communications, I've asked him to take on that role. Let's all congratulate Joe and wish him the best of luck!"

Putting Joe in this position would absolutely take best advantage of his strengths and passions, and be consistent with the second secret, *leverage*. Later we would implement the fourth secret by celebrating Joe's promotion at a leadership team dinner.

* * *

PASSION

A year had passed and the company was almost unrecognizable. We doubled our number of clients, hired twenty five new consultants, and expanded to an additional floor in our office building. We were also written up in our local business journal as one of the top twenty-five places to work. We were a fun, rewarding, high growth company.

Most importantly of all, we were a passionate company. And, after all those months, I realized that it was that passion that made us successful and would keep us that way. I woke up most mornings and couldn't wait to start work. It didn't even seem like work. It seemed like a fun hobby that I got paid for. And I knew that most of our employees at A.M. Consulting felt the same way. The positive impact that had on our relationships as a team and the relationships with our clients was revolutionary. It gave us a competitive advantage that drove our phenomenal growth.

There were some changes on our leadership team over the last year that fueled our growth as well. We promoted someone from within to be the new leader of our utilities and telecommunications practice, taking over for Joe after he moved into the director of business development position. And as our staff grew we realized we needed a full-time human resources director as well. We hired someone from the outside to fill that role.

Things still weren't perfect; however, I felt incredible pride for what we had all accomplished over the last year.

PERFORMANCE BREAKTHROUGH

At our leadership team meeting that morning, I announced another exciting change to our growing organization.

"As you all know, our growth over the last year has been a real blessing. However, our larger organization comes with added complexities and challenges. It's time for me to take a step back from the day-to-day running of our operations and take on a more strategic role. I decided about a month ago that I would start searching for a chief operating officer to fill the day-to-day operations role. The COO will be my right hand in the running of our business.

"Well, I wanted to announce to you today that I found someone to fill that role. He has a great understanding of our business, he's been a consultant for fifteen years, and, best of all, we stole him from our largest competitor. In fact, I think some of you may know him."

I opened the conference room door and in walked my old friend and our ex-director of business development, John Simms. Kim, Linda, Joe, and Rich couldn't believe their eyes. They all jumped up to greet John before he could make it all the way into the room.

John quitting and the loss of the Vault Communications account the previous year marked the lowest point in the short history of A.M. Consulting. However, those events also triggered an incredible journey that led us to where we were today.

I didn't know what would be next for my company or my family, but I knew we were headed in the right direction and I knew we'd get there with passion.

* * *

THE FOUR SECRETS OF PASSIONATE ORGANIZATIONS SUMMARY

Secret One - Acceptance

Accept that we're all different. Treat others the way THEY want to be treated, not the way YOU want to be treated.

Secret Two - Leverage

Stop beating yourself and others up for weaknesses. Discover and leverage passions and strengths instead.

Secret Three - Impact

Give people the freedom to get the job done. Allow them to feel ownership and true impact on your organization's bottom line.

Secret Four - Celebration

Keep a constant flow of positive energy throughout the organization. Celebrate your team's accomplishments, big or small.

* * *

A FINAL NOTE FROM THE AUTHOR

Taken separately, these four secrets are powerful, but put them together and your organization will be unstoppable. It will also become a magnet for tremendous talent.

A few years ago, I gave a speech for the graduating class of a school in New Jersey. The topic of my speech focused on strategies they could use to find their dream job.

At the end of the speech I asked them a simple question; "After you find a job, how many of you think when that alarm clock goes off in the morning you'll reach over, shut it off, and think, 'I can't wait to go to work today!'?"

Most of them laughed and no one raised their hands. No great shock. But then I asked them a similar question, using the four secrets.

"Okay," I said. "But let me ask you this."

"What if you found a place that knew what made you tick? They knew your values, your motivations, and your learning styles. They accepted you for who you were and treated you that way everyday." I asked, summarizing the first secret, *acceptance*.

"What if that same place understood your passions and your strengths? And what if you got to spend 80 percent of your time focused on those areas?" I asked, summarizing the second secret, *leverage.*

"What if they made you feel like a true partner? If you felt like they trusted you enough to take ownership and have true impact on the company's strategies, tactics and bottom line?" I asked, summarizing the third secret, *impact.*

"And what if they celebrated who you are and what you did everyday? There was a constant flow of positive and you actually had fun at work." I asked, summarizing the fourth secret, *celebration.*

"Would you be excited, would you feel passionate about going to work for a place like that?" I asked.

After a short silence, a voice from the crowd asked, "Does a place like that exist?"

"I'm working on it," I answered. "I'm working on it."

I hope this book gets your organization closer to that vision.

* * *

FOUR SECRETS OF PASSIONATE ORGANIZATIONS WORKBOOK

PASSION

What would be the result of a more passionate team or organization?

_____

_____

_____

_____

What's the consequence of not having an optimal level of passion now?

_____

_____

_____

SECRET ONE – ACCEPTANCE

What do you do to better understand your employees today?

Method	What do you do with information?

FOUR SECRETS OF PASSIONATE ORGANIZATIONS

What should you be doing to better understand your employees today?

Method	What do you do with information?

SECRET TWO – LEVERAGE

How do you leverage your employees' unique strengths today?

Category	Ways to leverage strengths
Roles & Responsibilities	
Training	
Career Path	
Recruiting/Hiring	
Performance Review/ Planning	
Other	

FOUR SECRETS OF PASSIONATE ORGANIZATIONS

How should you be leveraging your employees' unique strengths?

Category	Ways to leverage strengths
Roles & Responsibilities	
Training	
Career Path	
Recruiting/Hiring	
Performance Review/ Planning	
Other	

SECRET THREE – IMPACT

How do you currently create a sense of ownership within your team or organization?

_____

_____

_____

_____

How do you currently stifle a sense of ownership?

_____

_____

_____

_____

Potential ideas to implement…

_____

_____

_____

_____

FOUR SECRETS OF PASSIONATE ORGANIZATIONS

SECRET FOUR – CELEBRATION

When and what do you celebrate?

_____

_____

_____

_____

How do you celebrate?

_____

_____

_____

How do you play as a team or organization? What are the last three things you did for fun?

_____

_____

_____

_____

PERFORMANCE BREAKTHROUGH

Other notes/potential ideas to implement...

_____

_____

_____

_____

* * *

ABOUT PERFORMANCE BREAKTHROUGH

Performance Breakthrough works with business owners, senior executives, and managers to improve results through coaching, development, and planning. Their focus is on building the attitudes, behavioral management skills, and goal achievement processes necessary to achieve breakthrough results for teams and individuals.

They achieve these results by helping individuals and teams to:

- ☑ Create a crystal clear vision of what they want
- ☑ Understand what's holding them back from their vision
- ☑ Define and implement the right attitudes, goals, and activities necessary to achieve their vision

For more information on Performance Breakthrough, contact:

Mike Goldman
Performance Breakthrough
www.PB-Coach.com
MGoldman@PB-Coach.com
201.301.2841

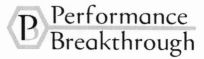

* * *

ABOUT THE AUTHOR

Mike Goldman spent seventeen years consulting to Fortune 500 companies and is now a writer, speaker, and coach in the areas of leadership, sales, customer service, and strategic planning.

Throughout his career at Accenture and Deloitte Consulting, he helped companies like Disney, Polo Ralph Lauren, Chanel, Kmart, Dillard's, Liz Claiborne, and Levi Strauss.

He is currently the president of Performance Breakthrough.

Mike's clients value his vast experience with organizations of all sizes as well as his incredible passion and energy. His no-nonsense, practical style enables individuals and teams to uncover opportunity areas and achieve revolutionary results with laser focus.

Mike currently lives in Paramus, New Jersey with his wife Angela, his two children, Richie and Jessica, and their Labrador Retriever, Rocky.

* * *

Made in the USA
Charleston, SC
23 August 2012